CPA
FINANCIAL
SERVICES

A COMPLETE GUIDE TO FITTING THE PIECES TOGETHER.

Great Fit. Smart Business.

BILLY HEMBY

DIVERSIFIED PUBLISHING
ENTERPRISE, ALABAMA

CPA FINANCIAL SERVICES
A Complete Guide to Fitting the Pieces Together
By Billy Hemby

 DIVERSIFIED PUBLISHING

Published by Diversified Publishing, Enterprise, Alabama

Editors: Mark Farrell and Jan Hemby
Proofreader: Russell Santana, www.E4Editorial.com
Index: Russell Santana, www.E4Editorial.com
Cover and Interior Design: Yvonne Parks, www.pearcreative.ca
Cover Copywriter: Dennis Welch, www.bearticulate.com

Library of Congress Control Number: 2022937451

Publisher's Cataloging-In-Publication Data
(Prepared by The Donohue Group, Inc.)

Names: Hemby, Billy, author.
Title: CPA financial services : a complete guide to fitting the pieces together / Billy Hemby.
Description: Enterprise, Alabama : Diversified Publishing, [2022] | Includes index.
Identifiers: ISBN 9781958331002 (print) | ISBN 9781958331019 (Kindle) | ISBN 9781958331026 (ePub)
Subjects: LCSH: Accounting firms--Planning. | Financial services industry. | Business planning. | New business enterprises.
Classification: LCC HF5627 .H46 2022 (print) | LCC HF5627 (ebook)| DDC 338.761657--dc23

Dedicated to the partners at PPC Financial Group, LLC

Contents

FOREWORD

A vision of leading CPA firms is always to advance our profession by offering timely and strategic services to meet our clients' needs at many levels. As a core offering, financial services integrate financial planning, asset management, and risk management with the accounting and consulting work that has traditionally comprised the heart and soul of our industry. Wealth management provides a mark of differentiation that distinguishes a CPA firm in its leadership capacity.

If you are thinking about providing financial services through your firm, there are several points to consider. First and foremost, the decision requires commitment. As with most worthwhile endeavors, implementing wealth management involves singularity of focus and dedication by a team of inspired and purpose-driven professionals. The mission must be clearly stated and adopted wholeheartedly firmwide. And all due diligence must be done to lay the proper foundation upon which a solid business can be established.

The proven strategies offered in this book can help you navigate your journey in developing financial services for your practice. With vision, entrepreneurship, the pursuit of excellence, and the right talent, a vital service offering can be created that will be highly rewarding for both the clients and professionals of the firm.

William H. Carr, CPA
Managing Partner
Carr, Riggs & Ingram, LLC

Preface

HD Vest broke ground in 1979 as the first investment corporation to offer financial services through a CPA firm. They established a network of accountants and brokers to generate investment, insurance, and financial planning business for their clients.

Vest successfully challenged the AICPA code, which prohibited accountants from accepting commissions.[1] A concern circulated through the industry that this could involve a conflict of interest or a compromise of independence. Surveys posted in the *Journal of Accountancy* indicated quite the opposite.[2] As it turned out, clients expressed more confidence in financial services offered through their CPA than other sources. This is largely due to the fact that accounting clients often consider their CPA to be their most trusted advisor.[3]

To successfully execute this business model, CPAs need to be willing to ask clients about financial services and obtain the necessary licenses and

---

1. Tina Grant, ed., International Directory of Company Histories (St. James Press, 20021).

2. Delton L. Chesser, Carlos W. Moore, and S. Sakarda, "Consumer Attitudes About Accountants as PFP Providers," Journal of Accountancy (June 1996): 181, 6; Accounting, Tax, and Banking Collection, p. 52.

3. C. Harrington, "Using Money Managers," Journal of Accountancy (January 2001:) 191, 1; Accounting, Tax, and Banking Collection, p. 55.

registrations for the financial services business. Some may seek to do the business themselves. Others may bring in financial services specialists while establishing a separate controlled entity of the firm dedicated to the financial services business.

Our financial services organization launched a practice as a CPA firm subsidiary in 2000. In the years that followed, we realized a high success rate in both business generation and client satisfaction. The key was not in associating with the right financial institutions or broker/dealer relationships, or even the best format of registered investment advisor affiliations. The key was in maintaining a reasonably high belief level in offering financial services as a valuable resource for clients and a significant revenue source for the firm.

CPAs often find themselves overworked and with limited time or energy for anything beyond their core competencies. The firms with dedicated financial services specialists enable CPAs to better leverage their efforts. They can generate a passive income source for their practice while ensuring a high level of expertise for their clients' financial services.

Numerous CPA practices—ranging from sole practitioners to multi-partner firms—can implement the business structure presented in this book. They can accomplish this in a manner that is easy to duplicate. If you are a CPA interested in developing financial services to supplement your practice, or a Financial Professional seeking to create a financial services business with CPAs, the chapters that follow can help you build a successful model that works for you.

Acknowledgments

A special thanks to Lou Bivona, who first introduced the concept to me, and Rich Engebretson, who championed the model and the broker/dealer firm where we first found success. Many thanks to the CPA partners and my staff who believed in the concept—and in me—and helped create the opportunity of a lifetime. Finally, a heartfelt appreciation for author Jan Hemby for her tireless proofreading of this manuscript.

Clarifications

I derived the content of this book from more than thirty years of experience in the financial services industry. In life, some lessons are taught; others are "caught." We learn from our successes as well as our failures. I have gleaned bits and pieces from both to benefit readers as they implement the business principles and strategies contained in this book.

For purposes of this book, **CPA** refers to both a title and professional designation for practitioners in the accounting, tax, consulting, valuation, audit, and similar disciplines. The certification of a Certified Public Accountant provides credentials that allow a professional to extend services to a multitude of different applications. In all regards, the professional seeks to advance clients in good stewardship over financial resources.

In the book, the term ***Financial Professional*** is a broad designation and encompasses many different approaches to work performed in the financial services industry. At different firms, titles can range from Financial Consultant, Financial Advisor, Investment Representative, Insurance Agent, Investment Advisor, Financial Planner, and many other terms for professionals who work in the business. Financial Professional is capitalized in the text to indicate a distinct title that could encompass many facets of conducting financial services work.

Prologue

We are rapidly approaching the apex of the CPA profession's offering financial advisory services in accounting and tax practices. This culmination of business integration when executed effectively can truly revolutionize and change the future of financial advice.

For more than twenty years, both the CPA profession and the financial services industry have faced business model challenges. With the right business plan and people, though, unique opportunities exist within a financial advice-based model that are both client-centric and comprehensive in nature.

What does this mean? Simply put, a shift is required in how CPAs and Financial Professionals conduct business together—from a transactional to a proactive and comprehensive financial advice model. Currently, both professions often cling to the "status quo." Financial products are sold to serve as tools to address client financial goals and specific needs. Insurance policies are established, investment accounts are created, and tax advice is provided.

However, thinking solely in terms of the current landscape does not enable one to stay ahead of the curve. Looking to the future, we are trending toward a commoditized client experience that, historically, has had the potential to produce either an element of division or a possible conflict of interest between clients and advisors. In short, between product promotion and objective advice lies a delicate balance.

From a global perspective, there are regions that already only conduct fee-for-service business. Work is done based on compensation derived from advice provided centered around a conduit for financial planning. In this context, the Financial Professional establishes a financial planning engagement founded on a selective menu of services identified together with the client. Business is conducted and services are rendered according to regulatory guidelines based exclusively on the scope of offered advice.

The direction in which the industry is evolving is conducive to further strengthening and making congruent the CPA's relationship with both the client and the Financial Professional. Here, compensation for work done is similarly based on time and expertise. Clients can come away with a sense of betterment due to identifying communicated goals that are confirmed as optimal and fulfilling from both CPA and their Financial Professional.

This book addresses many aspects of traditional and nontraditional financial services. It also provides insight into establishing financial planning based on the advice model to help the practitioner advance toward best practices. This is important not only for the present but also for the future.

Edmon J. Tomes, CFP*
Chief Executive Officer
Level Four Group, LLC

Introduction

One of the most profitable and rewarding business pursuits to establish within a CPA firm is financial services. It complements the existing traditional disciplines of tax preparation, accounting, payroll, auditing, and bookkeeping. Even more contemporary services—such as business advisory consulting, certified valuation, analytics, and assurance work—don't offer the same leverage of time and resources (with recurring revenues) as financial services.

The scarcest and most precious resource that a CPA possesses is *time*. It would only make sense that the most effective way to expand on a current business model, based on time for dollars, is to create one *not based on time.* Wealth management provides recurring income created beyond the traditional hourly or project labor limitations based primarily on billable hours. Any CPA firm interested in a more time-efficient revenue builder—that also expands on client services—should take steps toward offering financial services.

Most Financial Professionals spend a disproportionate amount of time pursuing opportunities to locate top-quality clients. When these practitioners don't make it in the industry, it's not because they lack the skill required to provide excellent financial services. It is often because they can't locate enough of the right people with whom to conduct business. Partnering with CPAs provides an optimal platform for establishing a strong client base. Financial Professionals can then invest their time meeting with clients to develop and sustain a vibrant financial services business.

A CPA firm provides one of the most robust contexts for creating wealth management. The CPA and the Financial Professional can leverage the CPA's role as a most trusted advisor to successfully reach a significant concentration of qualified and motivated prospective clients. When the CPA simply introduces a client to the Financial Professional, it immediately establishes a high level of credibility.

This book is a guide to creating a CPA Financial Services business model that can be profitable and rewarding for both CPAs and Financial Professionals.

CHAPTER 1

Deciding to Offer Financial Services Through a CPA Firm

Considerations for the CPA

First things first.

Are you interested in providing financial services through your CPA firm? If you think it would benefit your clients and provide you with a meaningful source of revenue, you may qualify as a candidate for incorporating financial services into your practice.

If you see it as something you *should do* more than something you have a *strong desire to do*, then don't do it. Without a reasonable level of passion, you will lack the drive to fully pursue it.

If you determine that your practice could profit from it, but you don't have a vision needed to make it work, it is likely best not to pursue this business.

If you have both the vision and the desire, the next step would be to decide if you should do the work yourself or partner with a Financial Professional. If you're willing to get the credentials, such as CFP' (one example of an industry-wide recognized professional designation), you may consider conducting the financial services business yourself. Before embarking on this, calculate the monetary investment and focus involved in completing that rigorous of a program. It goes without saying that it will place an additional demand on the time and energy required for you to successfully maintain the practice you have already built.

If you have structured your business around a few high net worth and high income clients, then you possibly could justify the time, energy, and money required for this effort. This may also substantiate doing the work of the financial services yourself, as this practice profile is not as time intensive as one that seeks higher volume and scale in ongoing business development.

On the other hand, you may discover that developing proficiency in financial services as a core competency is more difficult than you had anticipated. If you seek to create a gainful discipline within your more extensive practice—along with a passive income source that allows you to use your time more efficiently—partnering with a Financial Professional may represent the best option.

Considerations for the Financial Professional

Have you established your own practice or book of business, but want to maximize your efforts and expand your ability to reach qualified prospective clients? If so, you should consider pursuing a strategic partnership with a CPA firm.

In deciding how you would approach prospective CPA firms, think about what *you* would want if you were *them*. Research sources such as *The Journal of Accountancy* and similar literature to learn how CPAs think as a professional group. Consider joining a local chapter of a professional association to gain more understanding of what is involved in operating a CPA firm. Do this before reaching out to prospective CPA firms. This will allow you to communicate more skillfully and avoid the possibility of ruining an opportunity for business development.

Establish a working understanding of what you would be willing to give up in terms of revenue-sharing and style preference. The way you have conducted business in the past may change once you step inside the CPA firm. Suspend judgment regarding what you think would and wouldn't work. Your business flow may fit one profile, whereas the CPA firm's preferred business style may look completely different. For example, you may have focused on broker/dealer with commission-based sales. The CPA firm may emphasize advisory-based business through a Registered Investment Advisor.

Depending on your current insurance agency, broker/dealer, or Registered Investment Advisor affiliation, you may find it necessary to change one or more of these. This would depend on the CPA firm's agreed-upon preferences as you develop a business plan and confirm best practices. Changing established alliances can be a complicated process, so count the cost if you deem that it is, indeed, necessary.

Commentary

I have observed that CPAs identify and solve problems within their realm of accounting expertise. Similarly, Financial Professionals provide solutions within their realm of financial services. It is a complete package for a CPA firm to be able to provide clients with both.

Clients often discuss personal concerns with their CPA. These issues extend well beyond tax matters and cover a wide range of topics ranging from marriage and divorce to starting or selling a business. Often, clients don't know what they don't know when it comes to complex financial matters. So, they seek the counsel of their most trusted advisor, the CPA.

CPAs also want to know who *they* can trust for financial advice. They need a strategic partner who will consistently put their clients' interests first. The Financial Professional serves as an extension of the CPA and must demonstrate the same accuracy, effectiveness, and integrity.

This is what makes CPA financial services so successful. CPAs uncover the needs of clients who already have established a high level of trust in that professional relationship. Financial Professionals expand on that relationship to implement financial solutions. The collaborative effort produces an impressive success rate for business completion as well as a high client-experience approval level. A CPA in strategic partnership with the Financial Professional resembles a medical center with an in-house pharmacist to fill the prescription; the process is seamless and more efficient.

As a CFP® licensee early in my career, I looked forward to implementing what I had learned in my professional training to help my clients. As an individual practitioner, I discovered that I was spending a large percentage of my time trying to locate these clients—a common issue for any business in the beginning. (You have solutions for clients, but you can only hope for the luxury of having the time to implement them.) You first have to establish a large enough client base to generate the revenue needed to remain in business.

This model allowed me to take the time and effort I had previously invested in marketing and spend it developing a much more comprehensive business in scope and nature. I could effectuate advanced strategies for client solutions more consistently. The CPA partners identified clients based on their financial planning needs. This produced optimal business engagements and, thus, a high client satisfaction level. Client confidence was reinforced when they observed that I conducted the financial services business with the blessing and involvement of their most trusted advisor, the CPA.

As a Financial Professional or a CPA, your practice can profit from this business model without going into debt. There's no inventory, no warehouse, no credit line needed for product purchase, and likely no initial need for additional office space. And you shouldn't find a cause for borrowing to obtain necessary "seed capital." Expenses primarily take the form of licensing, basic support staff salary, and modest technology costs. This model poses a minimal business risk since the practice uses existing resources without significant capital expenditure. Since both accounting and financial services represent traditional and time-honored businesses, you would likely work with seasoned professionals with years of experience in their respective fields of expertise.

Op-Ed

This business is not for most CPAs and Financial Professionals.

Many CPAs exhibit skill at their craft as knowledgeable technicians. A smaller percentage of CPAs see themselves as entrepreneurial businesspeople. Accounting holds an advantage as an industry category because it provides a demand type of service—and a complicated one at that. CPAs acquire clients based on an unavoidable requirement for business revenue and personal income tax reporting.

As a result, tax and accounting professionals often need only to exert minimal efforts toward marketing and sales. They grow their practices through word-of-mouth promotion among clients and community proximity. In other words, CPAs cultivate clients over time by simply rendering quality service.

Most Financial Professionals begin with an industry knowledge required for the licensing needed to do business. Without some ability to actively market, the Financial Professional is afforded limited time to sustain viability. Clients *should* obtain insurance for risk management purposes, and they *should* make investments to develop financial resources for the future. However, unlike paying taxes, the government has no mandate that this *must* be done, and they don't impose penalties or fees when this is *not* done. If the Financial Professional can achieve survival of their business, then time can permit them to grow their business by developing a thriving client base.

The disadvantage of the CPA firm revenue model is that it primarily involves a direct exchange of time for money for all activity that the practitioner generates. The purveyed product is inherently limited based on the finite number of hours in a day. At peak times, such as tax season or audit season (depending on the type of practice), CPAs maximize those limits of time to the point of physical exhaustion.

The financial services firm holds an advantage in that many of the products and services produce a recurring revenue stream. The business model effectively optimizes time for money to allow Financial Professionals to render quality service and distribute their time allocation more evenly. For the most part, few hard deadlines loom that drive a disproportionate consumption of time and energy based on the calendar. So, Financial Professionals can maintain business development and client relations uniformly throughout the year.

A true symbiosis exists between the nature of accounting practices and financial services practices. Many of the Financial Professional products and services implement the income tax and estate tax savings recommended for the client. And accounting services business provides Financial Professionals with a ready pool of qualified and motivated clients.

A strategic partnership with CPAs also lends an even higher level of credibility to Financial Professionals. Since clients often regard the CPA as their most trusted advisor, needs and solutions provided through the CPA carry a lot of weight.

So, if it is *this* good, why aren't more CPAs involved in financial services?

CPAs must have an epiphany that a viable alternative to the traditional accounting firm model exists. Old habits are hard to break, and it is human nature to resist change. While there is no universal profile for any individual professional, accountants often approach business in a conservative manner and want to avoid appearing too promotional.

This can work in their favor within the structure of a financial services partnership. The accountants who find success do not vary much from their comfort zone or personality type. They don't suddenly become salespeople. They simply ask the client the right questions at the right time to uncover the need for financial services. Then, they refer the client to the Financial Professional.

Why don't more Financial Professionals ally themselves directly with CPAs?

Many have never considered it and don't know that the opportunity exists. Those who become aware of the business model may not possess a willingness to do most of the work for an equal split of the business. Except for the client introduction, the bulk of new business development, placement, and ongoing service becomes the Financial Professional's responsibility. Simple math calculating the time and expense involved in marketing and finding new clients affirms that the revenue-sharing percentage is *more than reasonable* for the acquisition rate obtained from the CPAs' referrals.

Other Financial Professionals don't pursue this strategic alliance because their firm does not have a format that would allow them to work directly with CPAs to develop a financial services business.

Financial Service firms could establish a limited means to compensate CPAs based on the number of referrals they provide. This, however, would not compensate the CPAs for the business generated from those referrals. As a result, this model may allow for the CPAs to successfully develop referrals but would not provide them with sufficient incentive and confidence to cultivate a robust business partnership.

If CPAs have obtained licensing for advisory business, the firm could establish a Solicitor's Agreement. This would allow some type of fee recognition with the CPAs for managed investment advisory account referrals between the CPA's Registered Investment Advisor (RIA) and the Financial Professional's RIA. This works if the CPA is individually appointed, or if the CPA firm owns an RIA as an entity duly recognized by the Securities and Exchange Commission with proper licensing and appointments for offering financial advice on an advisory-fee basis.

However, this level of affiliation may not be as substantial as a jointly developed financial services business model involving a dedicated Financial Professional with a full-time pursuit of business development. But it could allow the CPAs to conduct a modest level of advisory business.

The Details

In 1998, I attended an industry conference in Charlotte, North Carolina. One of the keynote speakers announced that the next wave for financial services business development would involve Financial Professionals partnering with CPA firms to deliver financial planning, investment asset management, and insurance risk management services. He compared it to a train leaving the station. His recommended course of action?

Get on board.

In response, I wasted no time in culling out all the pertinent marketing material at my disposal. I prepared a presentation that I could deliver at as many CPA firms as possible. I reached out to friends and clients who provided me with the names of their CPAs. Some agreed to introduce me, others gave me verbal permission to identify them as a reference.

Armed with brochures suitable for this mission, I contacted all the CPAs in my region—those I knew, and many that I didn't. I either showed up in person or called and asked to speak with one of the partners who might be available for a brief conversation. I simply identified myself as a local Financial Professional and referenced the

CPAs' ability to offer financial services to their clients as a means of developing additional business services and revenue. I asked them to consider speaking with me if they were interested. As a bonus, I offered professional continuing education classes and met many reputable CPAs that way.

Communicating with prospective partnering CPAs requires a "whatever-it-takes" mindset. The CPA culture is defined by hard work and long hours, and they expect nothing less from potential Financial Professional collaborators.

In addition, they need to observe a financial services network that will stand behind the partnership initiative. I established a strong belief with the CPAs that a system was indeed in place to provide ample support and resources to sustain their efforts. I even called in the top leadership team from the financial institution with whom we were affiliated. They engaged in discussions with the CPA partners regarding long-term business development and management.

It is important to note that I developed all of this outside of routine business activities to make sure production didn't lag. The fact that this pursuit had become a passion energized me. I was determined to learn as much as possible so I could be a viable resource for those who wanted to know more. A little enthusiasm went a long way as I sought to promote an interest in the topic.

The initial feedback I received from the CPAs was predictably mixed. Those who did not express an interest cited a perceived conflict of interest. Many simply were not willing to communicate with clients regarding the new services I would make available. A few expressed an interest and some intent, but they didn't follow through with the licensing required to fully participate. The CPAs who did show an interest had previously heard of the business model and had already considered pursuing the opportunity.

Regardless of the initial results, my efforts provided me with new contacts that proved invaluable in business networking. I discovered that displaying a positive attitude opened numerous doors for me. Even if a CPA firm didn't adopt the business model, they respected my initiative. I could see that demonstrating vision and singularity of purpose resonated with these practitioners.

Over time, I began to understand that the success of this endeavor hinged on my willingness to emerge as a leader and forge a path forward. Once I made that decision, I never looked back.

CHAPTER 2

Developing a Proposed Business Plan for Financial Services

Considerations for the CPA

Don't waste valuable time reinventing the wheel.

Based on industry standards of best practices, survey what other CPA firms have done that has proven successful. Familiarize yourself with the financial services industry's professional journals by researching publications such as the *Journal of Financial Planning*. Write down what you want to take place regarding business style and revenue generation. Readily disclose your comfort level for the range and scope of services offered, but keep an open mind to what ends up working and what doesn't.

Develop a working proposal outline rather than a rigid *pro forma* regarding requirements or financial objectives. In truth, you don't know what you don't know, and you will learn over time how things really work. Coming up with a few guidelines suffices as a conversation starter regarding the prospective strategic partnership. Let the Financial Planner handle most of the business plan development.

Considerations for the Financial Professional

When developing a business plan, put significant thought and preparation into every item of your working outline. CPAs pay attention to detail and will respect a prospective partner who demonstrates this quality as well.

Include in your business plan a proposed schedule of activities leading to revenue generation. This carries more importance than actual revenue projections since the "how-to" determines the numbers. Present an organized system that's designed for easy replication—the trademark of successful and enduring businesses. Reference the personnel needed to make the model work, with a list of functions for each position. Outline expenses so that the business plan comes across as measurable and believable.

Start small and take a lesson from Wall Street business leaders who under-project in order to outperform their revenue and earnings estimates. Gross and net revenue estimates should appear respectable in order to make the venture worthwhile for the partnership. However, don't provide numbers that represent unrealistic or unsustainable goals. Put yourself in the CPAs' shoes and determine what would pique your interest you if you were them.

Begin with a generalized staffing model; later, with success and volume, you can specialize staff member roles. I started with one assistant who did almost everything from an administrative standpoint. I generated all new business and provided all communication in client interfacing. It became clear when I needed to bring in additional staff. You will be able to specify the type of support required once any single category becomes too much to carry.

The magnitude and success rate of business development determine the different phases of the practice's life cycle. Your model may or may not involve all the components of a more comprehensive financial services business model. The staffing progression will vary based on the type of business you conduct. You may choose a narrower niche that requires less staffing and support resources, or you may pursue multiple disciplines of financial services that prove more labor-intensive. Make these decisions in partnership with the CPAs.

Commentary

When I was competing with numerous other Financial Professionals to establish a strategic partnership with the CPA firm, a major contributing factor for my securing the relationship was that I provided a written business plan. It was basic—but thorough—and primarily demonstrated how the firm could generate business and successfully implement an organized system.

The logistics specifically applied to that CPA firm, its personnel, and locations. Additionally, the tenor of the plan fell within the firm's culture. In other words, it didn't require them to depart from their established style. They could be themselves in pursuing business, and they were comfortable with that. I carefully used conciliatory and deferential wording to make suggestions instead of placing demands.

Most importantly, I took into consideration the input provided by the partners as I consolidated ideas into a working business plan.

Most of my competitors didn't present a business plan. They discussed what they wanted without understanding what the CPA firm wanted. One firm expressed their intent to work only with the top percentage of CPA clients. Another sought to dictate a referral requirement quota from the CPAs. All mentioned making money, but I listed *how* the firm would generate the revenue, and I provided a clear illustration to support the figures. I specified by product and service the percentage derived from the investment business and the insurance business. I identified how the CPA partners could obtain licensing and provided the basic structure for how that could occur.

A clear difference in the business plan I offered versus the competition was my willingness to build a partnership within the CPA firm. The CPAs would own a controlling share of the entity. An agreement of ownership participation existed for every partner within the limited liability company (LLC) we would create. The competition only spoke of an extraneous referral relationship. The model I presented was organic to the CPA firm's culture.

The equity partnership structure we eventually established differed from the income partnership. The CPA partners and I split income and expenses and distributed profits accordingly. I faced criticism externally from my peers and consultants for this type of business split. In this model, the CPA simply made the client referral and managed the client relationship. As the Financial Professional, I did all the work to establish the financial services business.

I was happy to do the work and split the profits. The most challenging part of the financial services business entailed finding qualified and motivated clients. If the CPA partners could provide the right people, I was glad to provide the right solutions.

The CPA firm's financial services subsidiary provided a passive way for the CPAs to further maximize their time and efforts, satisfy their clients' financial services needs internally, and generate additional current and future revenue. It enhanced profitability and increased the firm's net worth in terms of current business valuation.

It also established future valuation for each partner as they could receive additional income in retirement from ongoing financial services revenue. Alternatively, CPA partners could sell their interest in the LLC as part of a succession plan or a potential merger/acquisition and realize value at the point of retirement. In all regards, the CPA firm inherently gained value because of financial services.

Perhaps the best part of the business model was that it required very little startup capital or debt. I simply brought my staff and equipment and colocated inside the CPA firm. We agreed to pay rent to the CPA firm to provide them with an income stream. Even with that expense, consolidating offices helped us to realize a significant savings on utilities and numerous other costs. We earmarked that money for additional staffing, more proactive resources, and better capital utilization.

The financial services business can also serve as a valuable source of referrals to CPA firms by introducing existing financial services clients to the CPAs for accounting services. The Financial Professional's ongoing marketing efforts can regularly generate new clients for the CPA firm. Once the CPAs and the Financial Professional establish the strategic partnership, the financial services group can then begin to emphasize the financial services business for the accounting clients.

The Financial Professional must also pursue business development outside the CPA firm by continuing to network in the various circles developed prior to the partnership. This promotes a healthy, outward focus and uncovers new opportunities.

I initially wanted to supply at least 10% of the business from my own initiatives. At the time we developed the CPA strategic partnership, fourteen of our CPA partners had obtained licensing and had gone through the proper onboarding process. We operated out of ten locations, and on average, each location produced $1 million of gross accounting revenue each year.

My first goal was for our production unit to generate revenue similar to one of the office locations of the accounting firm. I wanted to maintain the same stature as one of the accounting firm branch offices. The CPA partners respected that, and I avoided the appearance of simply looking for a handout. I gained credibility by developing business through community involvement, public and private instructional seminars, and client referrals.

Op-Ed

Have a business plan and win, or don't have a business plan and lose.

After winning the partnership with the CPA firm where I was competing with numerous other financial professional candidates, the Managing Partner CPA for the firm confided in me that I was the only one who presented a business plan for review. In hindsight, I must admit it was a rough draft. But I put it together with great enthusiasm and heart since I wanted to make every effort to secure the relationship. What I lacked in knowledge, I made up for in zeal. I learned that exhibiting a sense of mission (more than *commission*) sets the right tone and builds a foundation that can last.

The Financial Professional should take the lead in developing a business plan. I recommend gathering ideas from prototype models and then personalizing them for the CPA firm's profile. The business plan should appear professional but still customized and believable for the formation of the strategic partnership. Write from your heart what you would like to see happen; leaders prefer genuine inspiration over generic rhetoric.

When interviewing a CPA firm, ask objective and subjective questions to avoid missing subtle issues. They will be drawn to what they want to do and will avoid what they don't want to do. Clarify key points to determine their preferences.

Do not start with financial projections; they represent the result of a successful business plan. Instead, spend most of your energy spelling out the categories for business development. Indicate whether you would emphasize investment business, insurance business, or financial planning. Show the anticipated mix the practice should pursue, then illustrate logistically how they can successfully accomplish this. Include staffing, scheduling, meeting format, location, and explain who does what.

When formulating a forecast for revenue and expenses, provide reasonable estimates that are within reach. You will find it easier to revise guidance upward and build on comparisons each year when developing a budget. Distinguish between the projected revenue earned from when you first place a piece of business and the recurring revenue earned once the business has been established.

Identify the financial services companies and investment platforms used in conducting business. This provides the CPAs with insight into where business transactions are processed. Detail the sequencing of reports, updates, and communication that the CPAs can expect to receive from these companies through the course of a year.

The Details

My early business model rough drafts appeared quite rough indeed. But each writing helped me identify what the CPAs sought in a successful business endeavor. I used a business plan to start the discussion. A profit and loss budget spreadsheet provided a point of reference for achievable financial goals based on the size of the CPA firm and the number of CPA partners. I customized the rough drafts to each CPA firm I interviewed.

Financial Professionals often assume that more information is better. But sometimes less is more. An ideal presentation is one that contains a few salient points offered in summary, followed by an opportunity for questions and answers. CPAs rarely demonstrate an eagerness to break away from billable work for financial services discussion. Inquire as to when they are conducting a meeting and become one of the brief components on the agenda.

I quickly learned the difference between insightful "intel" and too much information. I also learned that most CPA partners did not want me to distribute handouts and reports at our meetings; their offices already overflowed with paperwork. Concise, cogent presentations marked the order of the day. The partners valued that I arrived well-prepared to handle all the financial services details since they found themselves submerged in their own universe of details in managing their accounting work. CPAs like to stay informed, but more specifically, want you to stay informed on their behalf.

Remember that, in the end, financial services are a portfolio holding of the CPA firm. The income represents a dividend earned with minimal effort on the part of the CPAs. The Financial Professional is like the portfolio manager for an investment account. Involvement is good, but results are better. Just as investment clients like to be informed— but mostly want profitable investments—CPA partners appreciate the input but primarily seek profitable returns for their investment of time, money, and energy. The rewards come in the form of income derived from participation in the financial services group.

I also wanted to demonstrate a business model that could be replicated in any context, a concept many personal service businesses fail to incorporate. They often base business sustainability on a unique and, unfortunately, nontransferable personality. Any practitioner's departure can result in the loss of clients (especially when there is an internal division). But when you have a sound business system in place, you can conserve client accounts through the seamless integration of a new team member. Enthusiasm fades and personalities are temporary, but proven systems endure.

A *Business Summary Plan* reflects a statement of intent regarding the overall direction for the business initiative. It distills the intended tone of business development down to a virtual, one-page snapshot. The initial proposal should only display one year to avoid assumption and to keep expectations well-managed. More opportunities for extended projections will surface later after you have established fundamental success and cultivated an appetite for further expansion. This creates a buy-in from the partners as you begin the initial phase of forming the strategic partnership.

Production Unit Notes puts a little more "meat on the bones" and can help partners better understand many of the essential aspects involved in sound practice management. While it, too, comes across as understated, it focuses more on the core components you will need to address.

Client segmentation represents one of these components. Client segmentation provides an awareness of prioritizing client scheduling based on revenue generation and service demand. Another component is fee schedules for advisory accounts. These indicate organization and competitiveness among peer and rival firms.

When meeting with a prospective CPA firm, cover a range of services to showcase the well-rounded offerings available through the financial services subsidiary. This sends a clear message that a full-service firm is truly in place. Explain business processes so that prospective partners can understand how the practice can reach its goals and carry out the mission. References to marketing, recruiting, business development and management affirm the long-term viability of the practice. Partners want to know that this venture will allow them to capture current income and realize asset retention and disposition in the years to come.

CHAPTER 3

Finding the Right Fit for the CPA Firm and the Financial Professional

Considerations for the CPA

Examine your current firm profile to identify who you really are. If the bulk of your practice consists of middle and upper-middle income clients—and you are experiencing success—then craft your financial services business model to those clients.

Many CPA firms try to change or upscale to pursue higher-net-worth clients. Others may attempt to modify their culture and, in the process, lose momentum and focus. Numerous solid and reliable clients who remain loyal through good times and bad fare better than a few high-net-worth clients who are pursued by all the competition. The streams of income from ongoing client fees will likely remain in place when "trophy" clients change firms. Whether this occurs because of personnel turnover, a death, or a competing firm using an aggressive bid to lure them away, it could put your practice at risk.

The Financial Professional you select should blend in with your firm's culture. Diversification can complement your practice if you find someone who balances your disposition. Primarily, find a Financial Professional who extends the work ethic and philosophy you have established with your clients over the years. You want to feel confident that the financial services will serve as a continuation of what you have successfully executed through your practice.

Make sure you can comfortably relate with this individual. If you have a notion that something is "off," pay attention to that—like an aftertaste from eating or drinking something that tells you all is not as it should be. Pinpointing the reason may allude you, but continuing with that person could prove to be problematic over time.

You should enjoy spending time conversing with the Financial Professional candidate; they should "speak your language." (If they speak your language, they will probably speak the language of your clients as well.)

Clients feel reassured when they see the CPA and the Financial Professional working together. It is often the case that the CPA and the Financial Professional differ in style and personality. This achieves a balance in the collaboration of efforts. However, an element of shared culture must also exist so that the client identifies a cohesiveness that is both inviting and productive.

Of course, thoroughly research the candidate's background as part of the due diligence process. Talking with a range of people who either know the individual or who have conducted business with them could prove instrumental in finding the right fit.

Considerations for the Financial Professional

As the Financial Professional, you should likewise do your homework. All of the prerequisites listed for the CPA would apply to you in your search. At the end of the day, your decision to develop a partnership with a particular CPA firm should be met with an overriding sense of peace.

Expect the process to take a while. If it didn't, that could indicate an over-eagerness on the part of the CPA firm. They may lack the preparedness required to assemble a strategic partnership. You don't want them "cutting their teeth" on you as they make their way in a bumpy fashion through the learning process.

And you shouldn't appear too eager either. While "selling yourself," don't try too hard. You want to send the message that you operate a solid and self-sustaining practice, with or without the formation of a strategic partnership. Strive for that delicate balance of showing a genuine interest without looking desperate.

Continue with your existing practice as you always have while you cultivate relationships with prospective CPA firms. Consider the pursuit to be an additional business to add to your primary one. This will maintain cash flow and keep you current in the industry. Some practitioners make the mistake of disrupting their current business in hopes of quick results. CPAs proceed methodically and want to build trust and rapport with people with whom they do business. Don't rush the process. Prepare to build for the long term.

Commentary

Cultural fit is essential to most organizations, such as sports teams, civic groups, and industries. The strategic partnership I formed with the CPA firm worked well because I fit with theirs. I spoke with the same vernacular of the region. I was from a nearby community within the heart of the CPA firm's footprint. The CPAs felt that I wouldn't be viewed as an outsider to their client base, but as an extension of their culture. Many times, we knew the same people and quickly established a common point of reference.

Within the different locations of the firm, various subcultures existed with slight variations. It was vital for me to identify local heritage and colloquialisms to "get it right" in conversation. I held the distinct advantage of coming in from out of town—but not *too* far out of town—to avoid being perceived as estranged from the local way of life. I still had to earn my own credibility, but the CPAs' endorsement enabled me to earn it more quickly.

I found it refreshing to travel to a different location every day. Doing so enabled me to avoid feeling stuck in a rut. Even the office staff at each of the branch locations perceived me as a welcome guest. Arriving with fresh ideas and warm conversation, I attempted to add a bit of character to the atmosphere.

This paved the way for me to become better acquainted with the office personnel. These support staff employees often become clients, not to mention excellent referral sources. As a rule, they can also provide valuable insight regarding the cultural nuances of the office and the local community. Befriend these team members. They will often assist you with printing forms, communicating with clients waiting in the lobby while you finish a prior meeting, and completing numerous other tasks. Treat them with great respect. Learn their names and their family members' names and maintain an interest in their well-being. Most importantly, consistently thank them for their help.

Maintain a firm grasp of the concept that the Financial Professional is a guest in the CPA firm. This avoids your developing a sense of entitlement or familiarity counterproductive to the CPA firm culture. Remember that you are there to serve.

Even though you're in the financial services business, avoid going around with dollar signs in your eyes. People notice when someone is simply in it for the money to the point of compromising essential tenets of genuine business relationships. When you experience moments of frustration, go back to your existing support network for input and to vent when needed. The CPA partners are looking to you for leadership. Be ready to bring solutions and avoid being part of the problem.

Also, see yourself as a liaison. Often, CPA partners stay too busy to optimally communicate between themselves or with their partners at different office locations. You can provide constructive and time-saving updates as a trusted confidant. But avoid gossip. If you overstep your boundaries, they could consider you less than trustworthy. Nobody likes a snitch, and your reputation would precede you.

The CPA partners will periodically need to assess your work. Feel free to ask for their input, both collectively and individually. You will likely get more direct feedback from those who don't mince words. Take the criticism and reflect on how to apply it. Sometimes the input offered merely reflects one person's perspective, but you should still weigh it carefully. Negative people often see things negatively, but their input could contain a grain of truth that could prove valuable to your personal development.

Treat the CPA partners as you would treat clients. Many of them will likely become clients if you act as the in-house service provider for financial services. Their participation communicates to the other partners their level of commitment. It also assures clients of their belief level in the partnership.

As with other clients, find out what the CPA partners want. Ascertain this collectively as a partnership and individually for each partner. Hear what they tell you verbally and observe what they tell you as they demonstrate their life priorities.

For example, some CPA partners may want to retire early and form a path toward accumulating the financial resources needed to achieve that. Others may want to work well into their later years because they enjoy their career. These practitioners will likely seek to maximize the features of the business they enjoy doing and minimize those that they don't. Find out their reason "why" so that you can better understand what motivates them.

The revenue created through financial services may enable some CPA partners to maintain a favorite pastime, such as boating or riding horses. Those with children or grandchildren may apply the revenue toward a college savings account. As a Financial Professional, you can assist each person in realizing their goals, either through financial services products, or by delivering the sound advice needed to make it happen.

Op-Ed

The right fit usually feels right. Trust your instincts.

Not all Financial Professional candidates quickly emerge as the top choice. Sometimes the only way to tell if they are made of the "right stuff" is to allow time and multiple encounters to narrow the field. Nothing substitutes for due diligence, ranging from conducting background checks to soliciting input from peers and community members. In the end, you must perceive that you and your clients naturally lean toward doing business with them.

As a rule, CPAs don't instinctively promote themselves in order to cultivate new business and grow their client base. The Financial Professional candidate should arrive equipped to introduce that added dimension of marketing and sales and implement avenues of business development through existing client relationships.

Financial Professionals, by necessity, must be outgoing and oriented toward business development in order to create their client base. Because of this, they may possess a network of social and civic contacts that the CPAs have yet to tap into. Within the CPA firm's cultural context, the Financial Professional brings an increased awareness that cultivating new clients is vital to the CPA firm's well-being, both for traditional accounting business and financial services business.

In addition to displaying a capability to generate new accounting business, the Financial Professional should exhibit skill in developing the financial services business. They should possess a track record of success and a sufficient wealth of professional knowledge. Most importantly, they should display an unwavering commitment to growing the financial services practice.

If a Financial Professional is hungry to advance, they can quickly progress through the learning curve to achieve success for financial services delivered through a CPA firm. If you had to pick between prior experience or a willingness to work hard, choose the latter. Of course, you'll want to incorporate both experience *and* a strong work ethic when selecting the right person to lead the financial services group.

Ideally, the Financial Professional would have achieved success, but not to a level where the CPA firm's relationship isn't essential. Their client base shouldn't be so substantial that it would require a significant buyout in forming the partnership. If the Financial Professional has developed too large of a client base, those existing interests and demands could limit their ability to develop a thriving client base for the CPA firm's financial services business.

Hiring a candidate too early in the business development cycle may not provide the level of professional expertise needed for success. Hiring a candidate too close to retirement may limit the Financial Professional's long-term commitment to build the financial services practice. Selecting the right Financial Professional—at the right time—is essential.

This individual wouldn't need to conform to all aspects of the CPA firm's current culture, but a significant departure could prove detrimental to reaching existing clients. A practitioner who can establish good rapport with a wide range of people and communicate in terms that result in goodwill and business production represents a good fit.

To establish quality control, ask accounting clients for feedback regarding their experience with financial services. Timely input keeps all parties on the same page and helps ensure the development of a successful and enjoyable business.

When researching CPA firms for consideration, Financial Professionals would apply the same prerequisites. A common culture and a shared business approach are essential elements to forming a strategic partnership.

Expect to contact more than one prospective CPA firm; several may present themselves for consideration. The CPA firm representing the best match would demonstrate an interest and willingness to pursue financial services. Not all CPA firms will fulfill that criterion, even though they may pass the test in terms of size, scale, and location.

Of the CPA firms that do express interest, not all will put forth the effort to implement the components necessary to build a financial services business. In the remaining percentage, some will want to operate the business themselves without partnering with a Financial Professional.

Those CPA firms willing to partner with a Financial Professional will likely have other financial service groups in the running. To obtain a competitive edge, find out what the CPA firm really wants and present a model that best satisfies that objective. Prepare to invest a considerable amount of time and effort to advance through all the necessary stages of finding and establishing the right fit. Immeasurable rewards will follow.

The Financial Professional must fit in *and* stand out. Often the best leaders influence in a subtle—but highly effective—manner. They create an atmosphere of teamwork as they oversee relationship building and procedure implementation. In this way, no one places undue attention on them. Similarly, a leader should make an unmistakable impact on the organization by creating opportunities no one else has made available before.

The most compelling evidence of success occurs when all participants— including clients, staff, Financial Professionals, and CPA partners—move in the same direction and at the same pace with minimum intervention. A competent leader walks in unison with the group while keeping one step ahead. An indicator that the right Financial Professional is in place is when the CPAs find little need to involve themselves beyond essential participation in business development and periodic oversight of the financial services practice.

One of the first goals we set for the CPA firm emphasized the passive generation of income with minimal effort. A well-run financial services subsidiary operates quietly and unobtrusively to provide all participants with ongoing revenue. Timely communication from the Financial Professional at partner meetings and periodic advisory board meetings provides adequate updates and accountability regarding the organization's overall health and profitability.

The Details

I didn't know exactly what I was looking for when I initially reached out to CPA firms regarding financial services. I needed a willingness on their part to listen and discuss ideas. As with many things, hunger and appetite determine the potential for us reaching our goals. It didn't matter if they knew much about the topic of financial services; it mattered if they could develop a vision for integrating it into their practice.

A CPA firm that defines increased profits as the sole objective diminishes the likelihood of a partnership materializing. These firms would regard financial services as a dispensable commodity service if they did not achieve significant, immediate success. After a while, you can sense a note of resignation or indifference on the part of the potential strategic business partner. Be perceptive and trust your instincts.

If the prospective CPA partner appears over-involved, this could indicate your being displaced either before or soon after the structure's establishment. Some prospective partners simply want information to take and do their own thing. If you sense they don't view your participation as essential, make a note of that.

One prospective partnering CPA firm principal attended a conference sponsored by the broker/dealer organization with which I was affiliated.

They didn't communicate their plans for attendance, not to mention their pursuit of financial services business without my involvement. (Imagine their surprise when they learned that I was serving as a panelist for one of the discussion sessions!)

The managing partner of that same broker/dealer identified that almost all the registered CPAs—those without a Financial Professional partnership—lacked significant productivity. In fact, they cost the broker/dealer more revenue than they generated. So, the broker/dealer terminated many of the business appointments for those individual practitioners.

Growing the pie so that everyone gets a larger slice illustrates the goal of this venture. The pool is not finitely limited to an existing client base. A CPA and Financial Professional Partnership can repeatedly generate robust business and new lead developments. The CPAs can significantly conserve time—their most precious resource—to invest in essential core activities required to successfully manage their accounting practice.

A real test of the best fit occurs when prospective CPA and Financial Professional partners demonstrate a willingness to help others succeed. This can take the form of something as simple as providing client referrals. It sounds trite, but this can speak volumes regarding someone's character. More importantly, they exhibit it when they seek to promote the strengths of the prospective partner while extending forbearance for the prospective partner's weaknesses.

Another way to tell if you have found the right fit is if you enjoy each other's company. If you look forward to getting together for business development and client management, that's a positive sign. On the other hand, if the other partner mostly "gets on your nerves" or you dread scheduled meetings and collaborative efforts, you might want to rethink the relationship.

If you aspire for success over the long haul, take time to build strong alliances among the partners. Consider getting together socially outside the office. This provides enjoyment and allows each participant to see how others in the community perceive each partner, and how everyone interacts together.

Call it as you see it. If warning signs appear in the course of interaction, pay attention to that. It could be that your prospective partner may be skilled at what they do, but not the right fit.

Birds of a feather flock together. Differences among partners that complement each other can provide balance. But significant differences present the potential for conflict and could easily cause the partnership to fail. Part ways early, even if you detect potential for success. Though it may involve short-term disappointment, a better fit with the right partner could emerge over time. The end result will be well worth the wait.

CHAPTER 4

Developing the Best
Structure for Business

Considerations for the CPA

The best structure to pursue entails a true partnership between the CPA firm and the Financial Professional. CPA firms that seek to simultaneously form alliances with more than one financial services practice lack the commitment needed to make the business work.

If different Financial Professionals currently provide you with referrals, forming a partnership exclusive to one Financial Professional will most likely jeopardize those relationships. Perform simple math to determine if you can justify losing the potential business generated from those referrals. Compare those figures with the anticipated revenue you can achieve by forming a vibrant relationship with the Financial Professional of your choosing.

Having selected the right Financial Professional, the next step involves establishing a business entity structure and format. An LLC could represent the best option, as it provides liability protection as a separate holding from your accounting practice. And, for purposes of income and expense management, an LLC offers both clarity and flexibility.

Suppose the CPA partners choose not to obtain licensing for the financial services business. In this case, you must identify a suitable means of capturing value for the firm's added revenue and profitability. This could take the form of an eventually increasing entity valuation based on the elevated business revenue derived from the financial services business.

The firm would need to decide regarding when owners of the practice could recognize compensation based on the company's overall profitability. You would not base this on business revenue resulting from specific client referral business transactions. Direct payment from financial services business transactions would require appropriate licensing for each classification.

Alternatively, you could designate certain partners of the firm to obtain the various securities and insurance licenses needed to do business. Then, the CPA partners and the Financial Professional can split the business with clear payment directly from the financial services companies.

You could also devise a shared split of expenses. Each of the CPAs and Financial Professionals can fund the operations of the practice through revenue received separately in the name of each of the CPAs and Financial Professionals, respectively. This avoids possible regulatory or compliance issues in determining who is paid and how. You can allocate funds for expense payments on an as-needed basis each month.

Or you may create an agreed-upon split. In this scenario, you would compensate the CPAs individually from the established earnings before interest and taxes (EBIT) target percentage of the split financial services commission, or the advisory-fee insurance policy commission.

For example, if the CPA identifies 30% as the target, the split for all business could be 30% to the CPA and 70% to the Financial Professional. The Financial Professional could pay all expenses. This would avoid a type of pooling of funds between the CPA and the Financial Professional. If a surplus builds in the Financial Professional's business banking account, you could reconsider the terms of splitting the revenue. If a deficit occurs, the reverse could be true (after reviewing the expense structure).

For accounting purposes, decide if funds paid to the CPAs individually could be considered as part of doing business through the LLC. This would carry with it the intent of tracking business income and activity through the LLC, as opposed to having it paid individually to the CPA.

You would need to apply the same type of best-practice methods in this business—as for any LLC—to determine earned income from the business as a K1. Or you may characterize income as either W2 or 1099 active income if the entity is taxed as an S Corporation (if that is feasible), with an additional determination of income considered as a passive income distribution beyond the identified earned income threshold.

You may also want to consider paying the commissions to a created entity and classify the CPA and the Financial Professional as W2 employees. This works more easily if the strategic partnership has its own Registered Investment Advisor (RIA) and insurance agency. You can distribute the RIA investment advisory fee payments to the RIA owners. The same is true for the insurance agency's non-registered insurance product commissions. You would consider all participants—including staff and practitioners—as employees and pay them each a salary. The company would pay all expenses, including partner compensation.

By contrast, you could not as easily pay the broker/dealer's securities business commissions to the entity structure because of industry rules and regulations. Broker/dealer commissions could include commissions for individual securities trades, retail mutual funds, and variable life and annuity business. Based on the firm's complexity, the practitioners would need to decide if they would rather include or exclude broker/dealer commission product sales. You should pay those individually to each CPA and Financial Professional instead of paying it to an entity.

When starting, it is best to keep things simple as you gauge the amount of success the business achieves. You can determine the financial services business' profitability over time and justify further development of entity structures, such as an RIA or insurance agency. Broker/dealer industry regulations would most likely deter the strategic partnership from considering establishing its own broker/dealer.

Considerations for the Financial Professional

These details also apply to the Financial Professional. You would need to provide leadership in researching industry best practices. Identify the financial services institutions through which you would conduct business and develop a structure.

Like the CPAs, you must also prepare to develop exclusivity in building the strategic partnership. CPAs prefer knowing that you would not collaborate with other accounting firms for the financial services business, as it could provide competition and a possible conflict of interest. This may involve your disengaging with CPAs who stood to become potential clients and provided referrals. The same elemental math applies here in identifying any possible opportunity costs associated in dedicating business efforts to one CPA firm.

To begin the business relationship and make sure that the right fit is in place, you may find it advantageous to occupy office space in the CPA firm and/or pay rent for use of the conference room. This affords you the opportunity to verify the viability of business development and see what it is like to do business inside the CPA firm. It also provides a means of income for the CPAs while they consider becoming licensed.

You would pay rent even if no revenue is realized. And you would need to disclose doing business as "an office of convenience" at that location subject to the approval of the current broker/dealer, or RIA if you pursue security or advisory business.

Don't prepare business cards, advertising, or signage until you verify that the partnership will develop substantial business at that location. When this occurs, the registered principal of the current broker/dealer can establish an Office of Supervisory Jurisdiction (OSJ) status. This could allow you to move forward with the production and distribution of marketing materials.

You and the CPA partners could establish a professional service agreement when you set up an office of convenience at the firm's location. For use of the professional services of a receptionist, a local office clerical assistant—and access to internet, phone, fax, copier, and basic utilities—you could enter into an agreement to pay the CPA firm a reasonable and customary rate. This allows time for you to see how it feels to work with the CPAs at the same location.

From there, you and the CPA partners could determine if there really is a "going concern" to justify the next steps of licensing and the formation of a strategic partnership.

Commentary

The entity structure for the business depends on the size and scale of the business. We initially chose an LLC structure for the liability protection it provides. And with fifteen partners, the LLC format made income and expense allocation easier. Since the partners initially obtained licensing for all the types of business we would conduct, we found it was simpler to pay advisory fees and commissions to each person individually at the account level. When we set up investment accounts and insurance policies for clients, we indicated the commission split based on the percentage of involvement in the case.

If the financial services group generates general securities business—such as commission-based retail stock, bond, or mutual funds requiring Series 6 and 7 licensing accounts—be sure to pay commissions directly to the partner. In this way, you avoid appearing as if you are functioning as a broker/dealer by pooling commissions. You can assess business operating expenses to participants' bank accounts from the commissions and fees paid to those individual bank accounts. Set up a scheduled distribution for each partner monthly, quarterly, or annually based on the agreement.

We originally arranged to pay the Financial Professional more frequently, such as biweekly or monthly, since they derived their primary livelihood from financial services business generated in the LLC. For ease of management, we allocated a quarterly payment for the CPA partners, as their livelihood primarily came from accounting work. They regarded their income from the financial services LLC as a type of dividend.

If your firm has its own RIA status, you can pay the advisory fees from advisory-based investment accounts and fee-for-service planning into an entity account. This makes it easier to allocate expenses or distributions to the partners. Advisory-based business negates the concerns of broker/dealer–based business when it comes to income recognition and receipt. RIA ownership allows you to pay fees into the RIA bank account, avoiding compliance and regulatory concerns of commissions from commission-based business.

Your financial services entity may not have its own RIA but participates in the RIA of the same financial services company that has the broker/dealer relationship. In this case, you should pay advisory fees directly to the licensed CPAs and the Financial Professional since they all would have Series 66 (or Series 65/Series 63) licenses.

Our first stage of business involved participation in the RIA for the same financial services company that maintained our broker/dealer relationship. So, we paid all commissions and advisory fees to each licensed CPA and Financial Professional. We paid expenses, and then we distributed income.

The most flexible aspect of financial services business—from the standpoint of entity structure—is traditional insurance that doesn't require securities licensing. Term, universal, whole life insurance, and fixed annuity production does not require securities licensing. By contrast, variable life insurance and variable annuity production do require a Series 6 (or Series 7) and Series 63 securities license.

Some broker/dealers require securities licensing for fixed-index annuity production. If your broker/dealer imposes that requirement, you must generate fixed-index annuity business in the same way you conduct variable annuity business. Moreover, your broker/dealer may require the same licensing and business placement requirements for fixed-index life insurance that are needed for variable annuities.

On the other hand, some financial institutions may not require you to conduct fixed-index life insurance business through a broker/dealer. They will allow you to place that through a traditional insurance agency (not requiring securities licensing). Our initial business format used the master general agency of the same financial services company through which we conducted all financial services business. We paid commissions to each participant for life insurance and annuities, and other business lines such as disability, long-term care, and health insurance.

One more type of business to consider is property and casualty insurance. The two primary categories are personal lines and commercial lines. Commercial lines often involve larger premiums and commission payments, while smaller transactions with smaller profit margins characterize personal lines.

Before you pursue this type of business, decide *how* to enter this arena. You may find it strategic to partner with an existing property and casualty agency who has a proven client service structure, and who works with numerous insurance carriers through which you can conduct business. Service requirements may be labor-intensive. Therefore, you may not be able to justify startup expenses until you generate sufficient, revenue-producing business to sustain profitability.

Also, insurance carriers often require a certain level of consistent production before they offer an appointment for doing business with them. This may prove difficult to achieve in the initial stages of your practice's growth.

We partnered with local independent property and casualty insurance agencies to provide them with referrals. They, in turn, conducted and serviced business for our clients. We formed an agreement stating that the clients we referred would be identified separately from their other clients. Furthermore, our clients' insurance policies would move with us if we changed our strategic partnership to another agency or formed our own agency.

In time, we did establish our own property and casualty insurance agency by acquiring an agency in the region. This allowed us to develop and process all business internally and achieve higher efficiencies of time management, production scale, and profitability. The existing agency already had obtained the insurance carrier appointments needed to maintain a robust book of business. This gave us a competitive edge in all lines of commercial and personal line coverage. We were able to leverage our relationships within the current client base and attract new clients to provide greater synergy.

We decided to offer property and casualty insurance to our clients to complete the financial planning and financial services offerings for risk management. It strengthened our business relationship with our clients as it provided another opportunity for them to look to us for leadership in financial services. And, like other insurance, property and casualty produces recurring revenue for the business that remains on the books.

Op-Ed

The best business structure is the one that works.

In my search for a CPA firm with which to partner, I came across CPAs who expressed an interest in developing financial services in their practices but never fulfilled the licensing requirements and other processes necessary for doing business. However, the relationships still proved valuable in many cases. Often, these individuals acted as centers of influence for client referrals. They recognized the prudence of operating a business model for financial services within the context of an accounting firm, and they respected the high level of business standards this endeavor represented.

Some CPAs in my early search did not advocate financial services within their CPA firm. They perceived a conflict of interest in their making recommendations for financial services while adequately servicing their clients' accounting needs. I attributed some of the resistance to their concern of appearing too promotional in the tone of the client relationship. These CPAs never entered the arena of financial services themselves. However, they, too, stepped up as referral sources. They discussed financial services needs with their clients and then referred them to us for implementing the warranted products and services.

I also encountered CPAs who did, in fact, obtain the securities and insurance licensing to do business. But the time and energy demand of traditional accounting precluded spending time with clients to develop the financial services business. So, they formed an affiliation and became appointed through a shared broker/dealer, RIA, and insurance agency. This enabled me to conduct business with them and their clients, and we shared revenue evenly.

In all of these scenarios, the Financial Professional can carry out financial services business on behalf of CPAs. But in order for the concept to truly flourish, the CPA and the Financial Professional should establish a formal strategic partnership.

No one method works for everyone. Circumstances differ and styles differ. In my observation, the most successful model is where CPAs provide financial services referrals to Financial Professionals within their organization, and Financial Professionals conduct business on behalf of the partnership.

Individual practitioners require less systemization than multi-partner practices. However, systems usually make for sound procedures that businesses can efficiently duplicate regardless of their size. To gain insight into best practices, I recommend seeking legal counsel from a law practice experienced with financial services.

If there is one CPA and one Financial Professional, both will maintain errors and omissions insurance through the financial company with which business is done. The financial companies to which they are appointed would consider the CPA and the Financial Professional as financial services representatives if, of course, they have obtained licensing for the financial services business. The CPA would likely add coverage through the accounting practice's existing liability coverage.

Obtain legal counsel regarding the need to set up a separate entity for doing business. An attorney may advise you to create an LLC for possible liability protection as a separate entity from the accounting firm. This would serve to clearly identify a structure within which you can conduct business.

If your firm is a multi-partner practice, you will likely need a separate entity for potential liability protection and a clear business structure. The financial services business could possibly take on the same name as the CPA firm with the entity name "Financial Group." Or, to avoid an additional level of perceived liability, the financial group could assume the initials of the CPA firm. The financial group may even adopt aspects of the CPA firm's logo to further enhance the unifying effect. By contrast, the financial services entity could choose a name that is entirely different from the CPA firm's name.

Your firm must also decide the type of financial services business you will offer. For example, you may choose a fee-only financial services. You would build this business more slowly over time because of the gradual—but growing—revenue fee structure. If you include financial services products (such as insurance and annuities) in the financial services offerings, this involves commissions.

You will need to devise a structure for those commissions generated by financial services product placement. You could offer financial services products that receive more commission up-front as business is initiated, with less trailing commissions when the business is established. Or you could receive a commission percentage initially, and a residual fee that continues to pay to the representatives of record each year. Yet another choice is to receive more of a levelized initial fee and a similar residual fee each year.

We chose to include commission-based financial services products along with advisory fee-based business and fee-for-service business. We believed that the full range of financial services was required to meet the needs of clients. The implementation of life insurance, for example, fulfilled clients' risk management needs in many different scenarios. In short, we wanted direct involvement in all aspects of the business.

We also chose annuities as a part of our core products and services. The structured retirement income stream that annuities deliver often proves essential in providing financial security for clients in their retirement years. These products offer a compensation structure that allowed us to receive a portion of commissions initially as business was placed, and to continue to receive ongoing income to help with operations management and profitability.

Several financial services practices established by CPA firms elect to offer only advisory fee-based accounts for clients. This business model does carry an element of simplicity; no need exists for broker/dealer affiliations. The regulatory oversight of securities sales necessary for commission-based products differs for advisory-based business. A selective number of CPA financial services groups are large enough to justify establishing their own broker/dealer entities in the case of variable annuities.

A CPA firm deciding whether or not to create or maintain a broker/dealer often discovers that the demanding regulatory requirements make this unfeasible. So, financial services representatives maintain an appointment as a Registered Representative of the broker/dealer. But, when you are only conducting advisory fee-based investment, or fee-for-service work, you do not need a broker/dealer. The financial services representatives can either create their own RIA or become appointed as Investment Advisor Representatives of an outside RIA.

Greater flexibility exists in business development and revenue generation in owning an RIA since the CPA firm owns the entity. Advisory fee-based business compliance management avoids the additional oversight required of a broker/dealer business, and you can conduct business using an advice-based model.

The Details

Since an LLC provided the entity structure for our financial services partnership, all of the CPA firm's licensed partners who participated in production activity owned units in the LLC. We based their practice ownership on their pro rata ownership of the accounting firm, which was designated as a C corporation.

As the founding partner, I owned units as well, and I was the single-largest percentage owner. My original capital contribution was limited to my desk, laptop computer, and file cabinets. I also contributed one dollar as valuable consideration in establishing the practice.

Each year, all the partners received a K-1 statement to indicate income for the practice. Thankfully, my accountant—one of the CPA partners—prepared my taxes through the accounting firm. I welcomed the help as our K-1 statement was not a simple format to understand for income reporting. My CPA demonstrated a familiarity with the calculations and skillfully filed my taxes each year in a timely fashion.

For income purposes, I individually split 50% of the expenses with the other CPAs, who collectively split expenses. They based their percentage representation on their share of ownership of the accounting firm. The LLC's profit after expenses each year was allocated 50% to me and 50% to the CPA partners. For each account, I was listed as 50% of the commission or revenue generated. The referring partner for the client referral was the other 50% split rep for the account.

We created multiple split rep codes for me and all the partners to allow for full participation. The firm paid me biweekly the level draw against profits through the year to maintain a consistency of income. Then they issued me a quarterly "true-up" based on a rolling average of the operation's profitability through the year. The tax partners received payments quarterly with an annual true-up.

Paying income directly created clear visibility for rewarding each participant based on their effort level. It served as a great incentive for maintaining production level so we could stay ahead of expenses. (We always left a reserve in the bank account to allow for potentially slower times of business revenue and activity.)

The CPAs felt motivated by the recognition they received for their work, and a healthy level of competition developed as a result. Achieving a higher production ranking translated into increased compensation. And we could review the updated results each week since the financial company—through which we received fees and commissions—provided weekly production reports.

It all became real when money came in, and the CPAs' investment in the venture realized significant profits. Their percentage return on investment (ROI) was virtually infinite since they generated the profit with hardly any initial capital contribution. Instead of a cost-intensive business that involved a significant amount of borrowing to establish, ours remained debt-free. Our main cost was the time it took for the tax partners to maintain licensing and continuing education, and the effort required to spread the word to their clients.

My "cost" was to treat each client referral as valued and time-sensitive and convert each opportunity into established business. A crucial part of the work was providing timely feedback to the CPA partners and never missing an opportunity to thank them for their referrals.

For sizable CPA firms with a large number of stockholders or partnership members, it may not prove feasible for all of the partners to obtain licensing for securities or insurance. In some cases, the leadership may decide that *none* of the partners should obtain licensing if *all* are not interested in the pursuit.

For those CPAs without proper licensing—who do not receive commissions or advisory fees—you would not base compensation on the amount of revenue generated from the business established by the referral.

The CPA firm may own the financial services entity. But you would realize compensation categorically for ownership of the company. This would be to the extent that the financial services entity generates profits as a subsidiary of the parent company.

Activity for referrals could be tracked based on *making* referrals but not on the individual compensation of *business done from* the referrals. You could inadvertently consider this as an advisory fee payment. Or you could consider it as a commission based on business established for non-licensed partners. Realization of value for profitability in stockholders' shares of ownership or partner membership interests may vary among different business models.

A best practice could represent tracking business development (but not necessarily placement) so that, at retirement, you could realize the value in appreciated stock (for a corporation) or units (for an LLC) in the value of the entity. This is so that all corporate stockholders or partnership members would benefit from the greater value of the company as a result of all the revenue and profits.

Also, you could base a deferred compensation payout on a formula, such as three times the highest or last years of salary/draw of the stockholder or partnership member. You could also pay out an income calculation based on the total success and value of the company, including profitability from financial services. Often retiring members receive a distribution payout from the surplus funds in their "capital account" ledger maintained within the firm.

Some firms chronicle the stockholders' or partnership members' production activity by allocations maintained in the firm's capital account. They even provide distributions necessary to pay the income taxes on the funds each year that are recorded for the capital account, whereas the balance of the capital account funds would not be distributed annually.

Finally, the financial services' profitability could allow for the firm to maintain additional funds within the capital account to provide a larger distribution to the stockholder or partnership member at retirement.

CHAPTER 5

Creating and Managing a Business Development System

Considerations for the CPA

If you have determined that financial services could benefit your clients and increase your firm's profits, and you've made it as far as obtaining the necessary licensing, the next step is to conduct business. As a CPA, you can fulfill your primary role by listening to clients, identifying their financial planning needs, and mentioning to them that your firm offers financial services and solutions for those needs.

Simply say, "We do (that service) here. If you have a minute, I will get (Financial Professional). He (or she) takes care of that for our other clients and for us." Then introduce the client to the Financial Professional in person or by phone. If you can't reach the Financial Professional at that time, tell the client that you will ask the Financial Professional to contact them directly for an introduction.

Communicate that you believe in the services the Financial Professional offers, and, more importantly, in the Financial Professional. This will speak volumes to the client and will build a genuine interest and readiness for follow-through.

Make yourself available to either introduce the client to the Financial Professional or step in for the beginning of their first meeting. You could engage in a brief exchange by greeting the client in the lobby with the Financial Professional or by standing in the conference room doorway to confirm an overview of the basic facts of the client's situation.

This does not require much time, and it reinforces your strategic partnership with the Financial Professional—and your support for this opportunity. For more substantial client relationships, you may find it beneficial to participate in the meeting in a way that delivers excellence in advanced matters of tax, estate, and business planning. The small investment of time can better assure client satisfaction and business development.

Considerations for the Financial Professional

CPAs are busy people. They view time as their most precious resource. Let the CPA know that you understand that. With client introductions, listen to the CPA's brief explanation of the client's needs. Affirm your comprehension and preview a few details for resolution in the presence of the CPA and the client. Set up a meeting time with the client then or confirm following up to schedule an appointment.

After you've scheduled the appointment with the client, confirm the time and date with the CPA. It can be strategic for the CPA to stop by while you outline the details of the financial services conversation and the next steps for conducting business. In the client's mind, this affirms that the path forward seems reasonable, and that the CPA agrees with it.

From there, you would conduct business through new account forms, funds transfer, and all implementation procedures. In most cases, you can complete these initial steps at the first or second meeting. Once you place the business, schedule a follow-up meeting or phone call with the client to review progress and provide an update.

Provide clear communication to the client on an ongoing basis. While there are many ways to reach clients—letters, emails, tax organizer inserts, advertising, and social media campaigns—nothing beats a personal introduction.

Commentary

The first *order* of business is to get everyone to *promote* the business. If you cultivate a strong belief level in financial services among the firm partners—and properly motivate them—they will spread the word. The degree to which the financial services business thrives hinges on their full participation.

CPAs can introduce the Financial Professional to their clients during regularly scheduled client appointments. This produces better results than sending out letters—including financial services information in client tax organizers—or any other indirect means of client communication.

Business quickly follows. It can take a while to get through all the referrals when everyone jumps on board; you will develop structure around that.

This structure begins with segmenting your clients based on revenue generation and account profiles. Make geographical distinctions to enable scheduling to flow more systematically. If you efficiently manage the early cycle of business development, you can more easily refine the processes later on. Over time, you can initiate emails, newsletters, campaign promotions, and other means to develop and sustain client relationships.

Client outreach requires achieving a balance. Too much communication becomes noise and loses its effectiveness. Too little can cause clients to feel alienated or overlooked and make them vulnerable to the competition. Individual outreach is vital in this regard. Even with technology and media innovations, nothing substitutes for direct communication. This engenders familiarity and consistency and delivers a timeless message of care and interest.

As the firm grows, other service and production team members can build on the growth to sustain ongoing oversight and hospitality for each client. A model based on systematic scheduling provides the balance of contact timeliness with purposeful client review meetings.

Op-Ed

Don't complicate it. Just tell clients to speak with your Financial Professional.

It's not just what you say, it's how—and when—you say it. Base your scheduled communication on client segmentation. Relay this to the client through a Client Blueprint that you develop for each client.

This Client Blueprint provides an overview of important topics you will want to discuss with clients at regularly scheduled intervals. It's a narrative regarding the processes involved in establishing the financial services' new business from the time you receive the referral to the time you conduct business. You can modify it to fit your style and personality and to suit your local culture.

The dialogue is designed for a financial services partnership where both the CPAs and Financial Professionals are licensed for the financial services business. However, it can benefit all CPA financial services models. (Note: for a CPA firm that owns a financial services subsidiary but does not employ securities and insurance licensed CPAs, they should still disclose that the CPA firm owns the financial services group. The financial services business generates revenue both for the financial services group and the CPA firm.)

Though style and technique may vary among different Financial Professionals, communication with the client comprises the heart and soul of new business generation. Skilled dialogue in the form of information sharing, consensus building, and rapport development culminates in the execution of financial services business.

After you establish the initial new business, make sure that a member of the support staff contacts the client to welcome them, affirm the new business submitted, and provide an overview of new business processing.

Effective, ongoing communication between the client and Registered Assistants and Administrative Assistants would follow. The Client Experience Specialist would establish a recurring client contact schedule based on client segmentation and the client's preferences.

The Details

The best business development system is simply for the CPA to ask a client to speak with the Financial Professional about financial services. This could specifically address a need the CPA has uncovered, or it could represent a general invitation to discuss the services offered.

Nothing more is needed for the financial services business to get off to a great start.

A proven system of execution is for the CPA to introduce the Financial Professional to each client individually during regular client accounting meetings and phone calls. Since the referring CPA has already established trust with the client, the Financial Professional only needs to substantiate that credibility. The client must observe an authentic collaboration between the CPA and the Financial Professional to maintain confidence in doing business and enjoy a rewarding client experience.

In the course of repeating these two steps, the Financial Professional must establish a solid network of support personnel. As business volume increases, the Administrative Assistant role can be divided into new business preparation and client services management. As the Financial Professional further systemizes client scheduling, they will need an organized and winsome Client Experience Specialist who can ensure that both new and established clients meet with the Financial Professional at strategic times based on client segmentation.

With ongoing business development, the firm is afforded the luxury to specialize by discipline. The founding Financial Professional's focus and time demands will necessitate hiring additional Financial Professionals who can drill down more deeply on various aspects of financial services to deliver excellence in business development and client care.

Likewise, the roles of support personnel become more specialized as maintaining and managing a vibrant client base requires increased attention. With referrals upon referrals, the base will grow broader and deeper with multiple levels of client development. The addition of new producers and support staff will prove essential as the partners work together to perpetuate the organization and establish future generations of clients.

CHAPTER 6

Establishing and Maintaining a Client Management System

Considerations for the CPA

For the most part, the Financial Professional and the financial services staff assume the responsibility for maintaining the client management system. The CPA firm should keep its client data separate for reasons of disclosure and confidentiality. As a CPA, you should simply focus on reaching out to your clients regarding the availability of financial services within your firm.

Considerations for the Financial Professional

Your first step is to establish a state-of-the-art client contact and database management system. Segment clients based on location and account profile. Then schedule appointments according to a consistent client contact system. Provide the CPAs with an overview of your client database system.

You should train your staff in client record maintenance and communication management. Stress the importance of each staff member recording a history of client communication in the system. This fundamental step saves time and prevents an overlap of communication efforts.

In the initial phase of the practice's development, you would conduct client meetings and generate new business as you maintain communication with the CPAs. Your Administrative Assistant's job would entail scheduling those meetings, preparing and processing new business, providing general client service, and performing numerous other clerical tasks. As the practice grows, you can distribute these duties to other specialists in different customer service areas.

In the second phase of the practice's development, the Administrative Assistant would streamline their responsibilities and serve as the Client Services Manager. This position provides oversight for the additional support staff you would hire as the practice grows and begins to provide a broader range of services. One of the Client Services Manager's most important tasks would be overseeing the distributions of funds, such as account withdrawals and required minimum distributions from retirement accounts.

Since the first Administrative Assistant now serves as the Client Services Manager, a new Administrative Assistant could step in to coordinate all aspects of setting up direct deposits and managing client phone calls. You could also bring on board an Administrative Clerical Assistant to provide support for this role.

The Administrative Clerical Assistant would make sure that basic data, such as address and phone number changes, remains up-to-date in the client management system. They would field incoming phone calls and route them to the intended support staff member. They would also direct calls to voicemail when staff members are in meetings or on another call. In this way, they would function as the gatekeeper to protect each staff member's time. When needed, they can also provide clerical support to the Client Experience Specialist.

The Client Experience Specialist would manage the scheduling of client review meetings. They would identify client segmentation to maintain a rotation of client meetings, thus promoting robust activity for the Financial Professional throughout the year. The Client Experience Specialist maintains a crucial role in setting a welcoming tone for client interactions.

The Client Experience Specialist would also create client advisory review reports (required for advisory accounts) to attach to the client management system schedule for quick reference. This could include performance reports produced by the investment firm's compliance-approved, back-office support resources. If the financial services team develops a Client Blueprint, that can be attached to the client calendar as well.

Another position you would need in this second phase is a Registered Sales Assistant. This team member would offer support for higher-level functions required in assisting with client accounts. This position usually necessitates securities and insurance licensing to provide qualified client communication and administer varying aspects of market research, portfolio allocations, and account maintenance. This allows the Financial Professional to focus on client business development and strategic client-relationship management.

Again, you would most often require the services of the Client Experience Specialist, Administrative Clerical Assistant, Client Services Manager, and Registered Sales Assistant in the second phase of the financial services practice development. This occurs after you have experienced a measure of business growth and success. These new roles absorb the initial duties of the Administrative Assistant, and you can further revise them in subsequent phases.

Commentary

At first, we simply cataloged clients alphabetically and by the CPA firm's geographical location. We scheduled client meetings in proximity to those locations to make the best use of time. Later, we organized our client base according to a segmentation model and coded clients based on the referring CPA and the clients' business category, such as investments or insurance.

As we began to specialize by investments, insurance, employer-sponsored benefit plans and financial planning, we referenced team members based on their area of focus. For example, if we classified the client primarily as an insurance client, then the Insurance Specialist would assume the lead role and oversee scheduling.

We used the client page in the client relationship management data system to submit notes regarding case development and to store copies of estate directives—including wills and trusts. We also stored powers of attorney documentation and statements for different accounts, such as employer-sponsored retirement plans.

Bear in mind that the client database management system exists for the benefit of both current participants and forthcoming generations of clients and financial services staff. Build it in such a way that it can extend well past the lifetimes of those involved at the present time. If you sold the business in the future, for instance, having a record of client correspondence—as well as vital client documents—would prove essential to promoting operational continuity.

In developing our system, we found it challenging to choose which records to include in the database. With so many client conversations all year long, we could not make a record of each one. We decided that, if the information was critical to other team members for client service and future reference, we should include it.

Various leading client management programs can integrate with email and interoffice communication programs to streamline the inclusion of client communication. One team member can assign follow-up tasks to another team member for the different projects at hand. They can simultaneously communicate this with other staff members through email and other messaging media. Likewise, staff members can store documents on a separate drive as a backup to the primary client database.

Make sure that staff members can access all sites through secure means. This presumes that you are storing client files electronically. Some firms still maintain hard-copy physical records, but even those should be stored in digital, electronic format in the event they become misplaced or damaged.

Beyond the technological advances that currently influence client communication and data storage, practitioners primarily deliver client management through direct contact. The development of automation will increase in importance and magnitude since it conserves time and other valuable resources. But because it is human needs that remain at the heart of the financial services business, skilled communication and attentive care will never become obsolete.

A successful client management system can optimize the quality of client outreach. Team members can better leverage their time by having immediate access to client records. This assures clients that you have familiarized yourself with their profile and are rendering services on their behalf with insight and attention. Having administrative staff members, such as a Client Experience Specialist, to initially communicate goodwill, affirm their knowledge of the client, and schedule follow-up meetings, proves essential for client acquisition and retention. This combines human resources and automation resources to culminate in a dynamic delivery of client services.

The best way to measure the success of your client management system is through client feedback. You could do this through an official client advisory board that would span the geographical reach of your client base. However, that may lack practicality because of demanding schedules and the logistical challenges of convening in-person. Instead, simply identify a core group of clients to provide feedback on a regular basis.

In doing so, survey a wide range of topics on either a formal or informal basis. Obtain input regarding client care and client satisfaction. Select clients who represent a range of similarities and differences to avoid duplication of viewpoints. The best way to improve client care—and experience enhanced success—is to receive constructive communication from the clients themselves.

This input could cause you to consider new services or upgrade existing ones. The implementation of positive change ensures client retention and promotes additional business and referrals. Without a doubt, clients represent the most important asset of the financial services business.

Op-Ed

It costs little to obtain a new client. It costs a lot to lose an existing one.

In this business, few things cause more angst than receiving notice of an outgoing transfer for one of your client accounts. If you manage to reach the individual in a follow-up courtesy call, you may hear many reasons providing the rationale for the change to another firm. They may offer explanations such as a relocation, the need for consolidation, and prior loyalties. More than likely, the root cause is a perceived under-attentiveness on the part of the current Financial Professional.

The opposite result can occur when you establish a comprehensive and systematic client contact management system. This takes time and effort to build. Begin by consistently adding client information and communication and never neglect maintaining that with full attention. If you organize clients by segmentation and data, and provide sustained communication on an ongoing basis, they will remain loyal clients.

When you properly sequence clients for scheduling based on client segmentation, less opportunity exists for them to feel neglected. Even if you leave phone messages and don't receive a return call, they will know you made the effort. You establish a quality of belonging that is essential to human nature. It's like a club membership.

Be sure to store vital information and prior client communication in the client management system. This provides staff members with insight into previous client conversations helping them to knowledgeably communicate with clients. It also prevents a duplication of efforts. When clients feel that you know them and their family—and that you keep up with what matters most to them—they perceive that you are on top of things.

We all want our Financial Professional to treat us like their one and only client. A client feels highly valued when you singularly focus on them during discussions. When scheduling client meetings, the Client Experience Specialist should delineate a specific time slot that references a beginning and ending time, such as from 1:00 p.m. to 2:00 p.m. on a specific date. That way, you have communicated the parameters, and the client can plan accordingly.

You learn which clients work around a busy schedule and require less engagement time for a positive client experience, and which clients require more. For example, retirees often live a relaxed lifestyle. They enjoy the interaction and may not appreciate feeling rushed. However, clients who are employed—and may be squeezing you into their lunch hour—wouldn't like you detaining them longer than the allotted time.

Allow for a buffer in the schedule between client meetings. You could use this time to return phone calls or touch base with staff members. This buffer allows for a more enjoyable and effective meeting where you don't feel the need to constantly watch the clock. If a client feels that you have rushed the meeting, this could create a negative experience for them, and you could ultimately miss out on additional new business or referrals.

The responsibility of chronicling new business leads and new business development in the client management system lies with the Client Experience Specialist. They should generate reports that cross-reference myriad contact data points for optimal client database management. The Financial Professional Specialists can also monitor business based on each one's specific discipline.

When a sound client services management system is in place, the financial services team members can more easily access and disseminate internal reports. Some of these reports track client age ranges and geographic proximity for client outreach initiatives, such as monitoring or processing required minimum distributions for retirement accounts.

Financial Professionals often require various reports for client meetings. For example, they can reference an account performance statement and a Client Blueprint to analyze a client's progress in realizing key goals. Registered Sales Assistants and the Client Experience Specialist can collaborate in assembling account review notes and other reports for ready access by Financial Professionals. This contributes to a systematic approach toward creating an optimal client experience.

Administrative Assistants can prepare Client Blueprints and periodic review forms needed for managed advisory accounts that have a compliance requirement of at least one review per year. If the Financial Professional can quickly access these—and other essential client meeting components—they can offer the client their undivided attention. This type of systematization gives the practice the feel of a well-oiled machine with maximum smoothness and efficiency.

Support staff can readily access client data and prior communication when the client services management system runs well and is up to date. Clients enjoy cordial and inviting contact with all staff members who deliver a relevant and welcoming message, thus demonstrating their familiarity with the client.

Staff members should make it a daily practice to keep the client management system displayed on their computer screen. Clients calling in will take note when team members come across as attentive and well-prepared for engagement. This also allows team members to promptly add notes from their dialogue with the client.

It is crucial to have a staff member dedicated to developing knowledge about the client management system. This staff member will champion the task of staying current with best practices. They should regularly participate in vendor-sponsored webinars to remain informed regarding system updates and improvements. Feature them at periodic team meetings to relay any changes to the other staff members.

The Details

When we first began developing our financial services practice, we could only log onto client brokerage accounts and various directly held mutual funds. A few websites existed for annuity and life insurance business. With so little online access, we found it necessary to retain our hard-copy client files for reference. We have progressed over time—as has technology—and continue to improve client data and account information management. Our group has changed client management platforms numerous times.

In recent years, we dispensed with hard-copy files and transitioned to a digital file storage system. We continue to implement a paperless storage system for an increasing number of new account documents. Even when we do use paper, we still scan the records into an electronic format for processing and storage. Copy machines can also serve as scanning devices for statements, forms, and other documents to be stored in digital format and easily transmitted by email and file uploads to various team members.

Online signatures for client account establishment and funds transfer reduces shipping costs and saves time and effort. We can process checks remotely using the financial company's transmittal system for faster transaction time. The client management–system platform allows us to electronically retain most of this processing for our records. Our firm network also backs up data and saves it to a designated storage drive.

As our practice has grown, we have allocated a disproportionate amount of time toward technology support and development. An increasing demand exists for technological enhancements and updates pertaining to record and communication maintenance. The Practice Manager provides vital leadership in monitoring best practices with this ever-evolving dynamic. This team member must demonstrate diligence in communicating with staff and regularly intervening to ensure that a high standard of care is exercised with all aspects of client file management.

Top leadership must also incorporate client record-management best practices to demonstrate commitment and the importance of everyone's participation on a firmwide basis. All the Financial Professionals and the support staff must become proficient in using the client management system. The firm should address the topic at staff meetings and apportion time for ongoing staff development.

It's a natural tendency to resist change. But you must consistently embrace change, especially when it applies to client data retention. To stay current, look for new and better ways to implement technological advances into this area of your financial services practice.

C H A P T E R 7

Pursuing Specialized Disciplines of Financial Services

Considerations for the CPA

For the most part, the Financial Professional bears the responsibility of overseeing ongoing business development and cultivating additional associate Financial Professionals. However, you and the Financial Professional should collaborate when it comes to fine-tuning the financial services practice's scope and vision. Input from the CPAs regarding what each would like to emphasize—whether a smaller niche business or a full-service firm—is critical to maintaining vigor in the shared roles of revenue production and client outreach.

When deciding how to develop the specialized disciplines of financial services, you may want to consider mirroring your CPA practice. Determine if your firm fits the description of a general accounting practice: one that provides traditional services such as tax preparation, bookkeeping, and business valuations.

If your firm falls into that category, you may choose to build a general financial services practice that includes basic investment, insurance, and financial planning business. If you operate a single practitioner shop, or your firm consists of a few partners who share duties among a core client base, you may seek to structure the financial services subsidiary in a similar fashion.

If your firm employs multiple CPAs who specialize in different disciplines of the profession, establishing specialists among a broader range of financial services disciplines could seamlessly extend your existing profile. For example, if you offer the services of an Audit and Attest Function Specialist, this could mirror a financial services practice that offers retirement plan and employer benefit plan services in a commercial business or governmental agency setting. Clients who have grown accustomed to the specialized nature of the CPA firm may prefer a specialized focus for the financial services group as well.

Often a firm can command a higher fee for the specialized services offering. This applies to both the accounting firm and the financial services practice. It begins when you demonstrate a higher level of proficiency and the ability to focus more exclusively on a specific discipline. It gives you an edge over the generalist who may not possess the breadth of proficiency to handle more complex matters inherent in some fields of services. The perception—and the reality—for the client is superior services and superior outcomes. Clients appreciate the feel and the experience of dealing with a top-quality firm.

Your overhead may increase with an increase in scale, but so will the potential for enhanced revenue. Start with a general focus as you build the foundation for the financial services practice. Success and determination will dictate the direction of the business, and a mastery of the basics can pave the way for diversification later. This allows time for the CPA partners to coordinate with the Financial Professional to develop further agreement concerning expansion and emphasis for specific disciplines, based on client demand and profitability.

Above all, engage in the type of work you enjoy. What performs well in some locations and settings may not work well in your business. Where shared enthusiasm and common vision prevail, the probability of success increases.

Considerations for the Financial Professional

The business model developed in this book emphasizes investments, insurance, and financial planning. As the founding Financial Professional, you could initially handle all of these. If business activity and focus warrant the creation of the specialist roles, you can bring in additional associate Financial Professionals for a full complement of business development. The pace of development would dictate the progression of the different phases in the life cycle of the business.

You initially may emphasize a specific focus of financial services, such as investment business, and continue to concentrate on that as the practice grows. The Financial Professional who began as a "generalist" may develop a more concentrated focus as an Investment Specialist.

You could add an Insurance Specialist as a reasonable next step in what you may consider a subsequent phase of growth. The industry often views insurance as a demand category of financial services. This could justify bringing in an additional associate to augment the work of the founding Financial Professional.

A great deal of symbiosis can exist as the efforts of each associate compound further business development. Insurance reviews can lead to investment business, and investment reviews can lead to more insurance business. Having a specialist in both categories allows for more advanced client business development. Both roles integrate well with the work of the CPA.

From there, you can establish additional specialist roles. For example, to fully develop financial services to small business entities, you could bring on board an Employer Benefit Plan Specialist who emphasizes the full range of employer benefits, including group retirement and insurance plans. This team member could strategically reach small business owners as well as generate significant growth for commercial businesses.

CPAs often view closely held local businesses as the lifeblood of their practice. Consequently, you may gain access to a high percentage of these contacts through the CPA firm. They often provide new business development opportunities for employers and employees, resulting in individual investment and insurance business.

Partnering with Investment and Insurance Specialists can lead to success in property and casualty insurance. A Property and Casualty Insurance Specialist could add another dynamic to your business model. Property and Casualty Insurance represents a viable specialty focus. Both commercial and personal lines insurance can promote extensive business in all disciplines of the financial services practice.

The addition of a Financial Planning Specialist could prove beneficial as a percentage of clients will prefer an advice-driven financial planning model that provides quantitative and qualitative guidance. By offering sound financial planning, you can ultimately establish investment and insurance business for individuals and closely held businesses. You could then make financial planning a premier focus of the financial services group. Cultivating financial planning opportunities from clients with existing investment and insurance business could represent the best approach.

As financial planning develops, you may want to consider hiring a Paraplanner Financial Website Concierge to provide support for the financial planning process. They would primarily focus on developing client financial websites. This would include setting up the website and teaching clients, step by step, how to effectively use it for financial planning.

In yet another phase of practice development, you could add a Practice Manager to oversee all aspects of operations, compliance, staff management, and business administration. Initially, the founding Financial Professional could handle most of these duties. But with business expansion—including additional staffing—the practice's administrative needs may require a dedicated Practice Manager.

Whereas the Administrative Assistant could initially handle new business and client services in conjunction with the Financial Professional, you may need to create a New Business Manager position as the practice grows. The New Business Manager would handle all aspects of new account preparation, new business processing, and pending case completion. This would allow the Financial Professionals more time for business development and client communication.

The establishment of an effective team of advisors and support staff may justify your hiring a Marketing Coordinator and an Event Planner to organize client appreciation dinners and educational seminars. These team members serve as the "icing on the cake" as they execute attentiveness to clients that often extends beyond the financial services arena, such as congratulating them for community accomplishments and offering condolences during bereavement.

Commentary

As a Financial Professional, you will most likely operate as a generalist when you first open for business—it's a matter of survival. You may not have discovered yet the industry discipline that best suits you, or which financial services your clients will require. So, you look for opportunities based on the needs uncovered during client conversations.

This can result in a broad approach across the primary disciplines of investments, insurance, retirement plans, employer benefits, and financial planning. An advantage to this method is that it allows you to develop experience and knowledge across the spectrum of services. Later, when you expand your practice, you will emerge as the one with the most experience and knowledge of each discipline. As a result, you can provide valuable oversight to the Financial Professional Specialists as you add them to the group.

A growing practice sets the stage for team members to emerge as specialists. Each can rely on the other to master the knowledge required for their area of focus. Often these practitioners can advance as specialists because the founding Financial Professional laid the groundwork as a generalist.

If the partners conduct business through a mutual effort, make sure to create a fair split for revenue allocation. The firm partners should reach an agreement regarding the percentages allocated for different functions. At least four areas of involvement could exist: business development, research and preparation, presentation and closure, and ongoing management. You could award each role a 25% inclusion of revenue generation.

Some financial services companies charge an annual fee for maintaining numerous "rep codes" to identify joint advisor participation at the account level. The split business manner makes it simpler to account for fees and commissions received where the companies pay the licensed Financial Professionals separately from each account. Each team member receives income, and you can systematically access the financial services' business management expenses. All participants can identify the compensation earned and, therefore, track their mutual success.

Op-Ed

Take it one step at a time. Do a few things well, then add to that.

For the most part, the development of the financial services business occurs one client at a time by one Financial Professional at a time. If too many voices chime in, confusion can result. The Financial Professional can integrate an organized team of Financial Professionals as increased demand requires a specialization of disciplines. Even then, Financial Professionals acting in unison continue to conduct business one client at a time.

A CPA firm that possesses ample resources to establish a team of production and support staff should still start out with one or two Financial Professionals and a small core of service personnel. In doing so, the firm will benefit from minimal expenditures and a sharpened clarity regarding role fulfillment. They will quickly recognize which areas require expansion.

For example, a CPA firm that emphasizes small business tax and accounting work may soon discover that employer benefit programs and retirement plans represent their most natural financial services market. They would plan to develop those areas over other anticipated categories.

A financial group may perceive that certain aspects of financial services warrant priority development. But as they conduct business, they find that other categories provide a better fit and should take precedence.

Success in the initial categories of financial services may prompt business that flows over into other areas, such as employer life insurance and estate conservation. This may require additional production team members, such as a dedicated Life Insurance Specialist.

From there, the Financial Professional may need to delineate staffing between support personnel who focus on closely held business employer–sponsored plans, and those who specialize in insurance and risk management. For example, property and casualty insurance may become a vibrant category. In time, the need could arise for a Property and Casualty Insurance Specialist and support personnel for personal and commercial lines of coverage.

In this way, the form of the financial services develops as business demand and flow takes on a life of its own. This cycle represents peaks and troughs of profitability. At the top of the cycle, a culmination of business development for each business category can exist. Support personnel and infrastructure costs, however, can reduce profitability in the short term as the practice invests resources in supporting those business lines.

Within a cycle, one category can experience business development saturation while another experiences a decrease. This produces diversification within the business model since different business categories may flourish or lag at certain times.

As a Financial Professional, you may observe robust activity associated with investment asset management business during times of economic expansion. Insurance and risk management may emerge as a focal point in times of economic contraction. After the financial services practice has grown to where each category is represented, you will become more aware of the client demand for each one. This makes you better equipped to know which category's initiatives to emphasize going forward. All the financial services disciplines that you integrate can support the other disciplines within the firm's ecosystem.

The Details

Bigger is not necessarily better, but bigger often advances levels of production and service that *become* better.

When my Administrative Assistant and I first began working from the partnering CPA firm's office, the experience resembled moving into a new neighborhood. The environment felt refreshingly different. The accounting staff's daily flow of activity produced a type of background music—a steady hum that kept us all moving along at the same pace. The camaraderie and shared work ethic we enjoyed enabled us to plow ahead and get the job done.

Soon it was time to bring in another Administrative Assistant to focus on new business preparation and to allow the existing Administrative Assistant to concentrate on client service. To maintain a smooth and consistent schedule—and enable me to continue to focus on new business development—we brought in a Client Experience Specialist, and our team enjoyed a new level of efficiency. The practice then required a Registered Sales Assistant to provide support with all aspects of management and communication for existing client accounts.

This core group formation continued for a few years. The next level of achievement mandated our hiring an additional Financial Professional to focus on employer-sponsored benefit and retirement plans. This involved more on-site work to fully develop business opportunities for closely held business owners and their employee base. To fully support that endeavor, we also hired an Administrative Assistant.

We then added another Financial Professional to focus on insurance and risk management. This enabled me to specialize in individual investment accounts, as a growing demand required my increased concentration. We brought another Administrative Assistant on board to help the Insurance Specialist with new business preparation and client service management.

As members of our Administrative Support Team became increasingly specialized, they possessed less time to attend to general clerical duties. Therefore, we hired an Administrative Clerical Assistant to perform tasks such as updating client addresses and phone numbers, beneficiary listings, and other clerical tasks too numerous to list.

Financial planning and fee-for-service work represented at least one additional area that required expansion. We gradually integrated it into our service offering platform on a limited basis. But to fully implement it for a wider range of clients, we brought a Financial Planning Specialist on board to manage that service.

In my experience, fee-based planning requires an individual who can provide a different approach to financial services. The open architecture platform offers a refreshing alternative to specific, product-driven financial services solutions.

With most financial services, practitioners present tools, such as investment accounts or insurance policies, to meet an identified need.

By contrast, the financial planning process offers solutions that are not strictly limited to financial services products. It presents a divergent advice-based process that can extend to multiple aspects of daily living and enhance the client's overall quality of life.

With success, the financial planning business may also require a Paraplanner Financial Website Concierge to support the planning process. This team member would serve clients by uploading financial planning agreements, financial planning presentations, client deliverables, and other documents onto a complete Personal Financial Website.

This closes the circle on the first-generation financial services team model. The process will repeat upon the introduction of the next generation of production and support staff. The integration of successor professionals in rotation will depend on the demands and needs of the practice and the tenure of the existing Financial Professionals.

The optimal arrangement would resemble an apprentice structure where next-generation staffing remains in place for three to five years for training to gain client familiarity before passing the baton. Depending on the financial services business growth rate, multiple circles of overlap and participation could develop among existing team members and those who will carry the torch in the future.

CHAPTER 8

Financial Planning: To Fee or Not to Fee

Considerations for the CPA

Financial Planning on a "fee-for-service" basis represents an important topic in the financial services industry. As a CPA, you should decide whether to offer it through your financial services subsidiary.

In most cases, this service mirrors a traditional accounting practice where CPAs earn revenue based on a billable time model. The Financial Professional bills for the time they spend developing a financial planning case with the client. The Financial Professional develops a financial planning agreement for compensation, which functions like a client engagement letter for the CPA firm. In some cases, the Financial Professional charges a flat fee for the project based on the assignments required.

If, as a CPA, you participate in the financial planning case to provide input on topics such as tax and estate planning, the Financial Professional would include you in the billing fee—but only if you are duly licensed and appointed with the firm's RIA. Or you could receive compensation simply as an accountant. The RIA would bill the Financial Professional who, in turn, would remit payment from the gross billing fee.

If the CPAs in your firm have obtained advisory business licensing, you may find it feasible to consider them as joint advisors for the financial planning work. The RIA would then compensate the CPAs based on the revenue generated from the advisory fee.

The fee-for-service model holds an advantage in that it offers an enhanced level of objectivity independent of the traditional financial services business of product transaction. Once you and the Financial Professional have created a level of trust and knowledge through the fee-based planning process, your clients may consider establishing subsequent financial services investments and insurance business.

Some CPAs and Financial Professionals bundle the financial planning fee with the investment advisory account fee deducted systematically from the client account. If you employ this method, you must clearly disclose to the client the difference between the advisory account management fee and the financial planning fee. You would need to draw up a new client Financial Planning Engagement Agreement each year to clarify and confirm the ongoing financial planning service and fee payment.

Considerations for the Financial Professional

As the Financial Professional, you would take leadership to ensure that all components of financial planning services meet compliance standards and represent best practices for the client. Periodically check the expiration dates on required client disclosure and engagement forms, as well as financial planning tools and services, to determine if they are current and state-of-the-art. You would expect to advise both the CPA and the client in all aspects of the financial planning process.

Coordinate with the CPA regarding their level of involvement in the financial planning process and defer to them topics representing their area of expertise. For more complex cases, the CPA may choose to participate more fully in the discovery and presentation phase. Otherwise, they may delegate the scope and sequence of the financial planning to you. You would also choose which aspects of the process to retain for more direct involvement, and which to delegate to the centralized planning support personnel.

A dedicated Central Financial Planner or Paraplanner can assist with the logistics of data input, analysis, report generation, and website development. This frees up time for you to communicate and interact with clients. Certain tasks, such as which financial planning components to emphasize, would require your higher level of decision-making skills. You can delegate other tasks to the support personnel.

As the Financial Professional, you serve as the point person who interfaces most with clients. Client interaction strengthens business development. You cultivate new opportunities for additional financial planning and financial services by spending quality time with your clients.

Your high belief level in the viability and importance of financial planning represents the single most essential component in incorporating and sustaining a successful financial planning business. This rings true from the initial client conversation, to the financial planning processes and document delivery, all the way to confirming and collecting the planning fee. If you or the CPA lack a sense of conviction, it can cause the client to feel reluctant, and business will not reach its full potential.

Conversely, if you and the CPA demonstrate a solidarity of thought and vision, this will be shared by the client resulting in a positive experience for everyone involved.

Financial planning is a methodical process. It requires that you use a systematic approach to client development and advice delivery. A popular adage states that "the devil is in the details." In this case, the "devil" would be in *not paying attention to the details*. Myriad detailed processes follow the initial engagement. The firm's RIA would need to provide clients with all the forms required for the financial planning engagement process.

Some clients will approach financial planning in a progressive manner. They may begin with a basic format, such as setting up a Personal Financial Website. This could serve as the best starting point as it would provide you with a snapshot of their current financial situation. From there, these clients may proceed to discussing more comprehensive financial planning and fee-for-service work.

Talking points should follow along the same lines for clients who have expressed an interest in financial planning but who hesitate agreeing to a more time-intensive or cost-intensive commitment. Often, one of the Financial Professional Specialists would engage these clients first. Based on the initial discussion, they would then make a referral to the Financial Professional either in person or through a conference call.

Commentary

Financial planning practitioners possess a recognizable passion for the business. With near missionary zeal, they engage in a constant search for like-minded clients or potential "converts" to whom they can introduce a type of work that offers more of an objective approach.

The Financial Planning Specialist endeavors to deliver unbiased advice based on quantitative reporting. Clients who prefer seeing a variety of scenarios find this particularly useful. The Financial Planning Specialist can also produce a "deliverable" report to illustrate current resources and asset allocation in executing potential outcomes for the client.

To further enhance client service, the Financial Planning Specialist can create a model for executing financial planning projects like the one that the accounting practice uses. This could include a larger-scale development of a comprehensive financial plan, or smaller-scale research work based on a client's specific topics of interest. Financial planners often base their billing on an hourly rate. Alternatively, they can estimate their fees based on the financial planning assignment.

Often, the fee-for-service model does not rely upon the client doing financial services business in conjunction with the financial plan. It's often stated in the industry that, in this context, the CPA offers the diagnosis and the Financial Planning Specialist "writes the prescription." The client then chooses who will "fill the prescription" to establish the investment portfolio or the insurance coverage needed to meet the financial plan's objectives. Affirm to the client that the Financial Planning Specialist highly recommends your "in-house pharmacy."

The Financial Planning Specialist may advise the client to invest. If the Financial Professional is part of an investment advisory group, the Financial Professional can discuss investing with the client according to the financial plan.

If the investment work involves an advisory account platform, the advisor completes the work and provides consultation based on the advice model. They should ensure that the process adheres to the advisory business guidelines issued by the Securities and Exchange

Commission. This type of business execution requires Series 66 (or Series 65/63) licensing.

The investment advisory account management work is based on a percentage of assets under management where the account generates the advisory fees. Alternatively, some practitioners could simply bill for the work based on a Financial Planning Agreement. In this case, the client pays the fee directly. In both examples, the "product" represents the advice offered instead of a financial services product.

Many advisors offer a range of services that include both investment assets under management, and fee-for-service financial planning. Both of these services require a fee schedule from the advisor.

For investment assets under management, the advisor can charge from a range of percentages. Some advisors tier the fees based on the size of the investment account. The first range of investment account balances present at a higher fee. The fees of the ascending tier levels get progressively lower. Others charge the same fee for all assets, while still others recognize breakpoints for the entire account at certain size levels.

The investment advisory agreement for client accounts would indicate the fee schedule. The advisor discloses the fees in discussion with the client while forming an agreement for setting up the account. The advisor provides Form ADV Part II A (for the advisory firm) and Part II B (for the individual advisors) to the client. If the advisory fee includes financial planning work, the advisor must disclose this.

The advisor would complete the planning agreement each year for the client. This would show that they are providing the financial planning service at no additional fee besides the percentage fee referenced in the investment advisory agreement. For fee-for-service work, the financial planning agreement indicates the scope and specific modules that the advisor will perform upon completion of the financial plan.

Some firms require that clients pay in full for the financial plans upfront. Other firms may require clients to pay a portion upfront and then another portion mid-plan. Still others choose not to receive any compensation until they have completed the plan and delivered the financial planning reports, if they have generated deliverable reports.

Some advisors operate on a retainer basis for on-demand work performed on a recurring basis, while others work on a recurring basis for identified modules for the financial plan.

Cases exist where the advisor establishes a bank draft or debit from the investment account (for non-retirement accounts) for recurring fee payments. They will utilize billing and collections if they invoice clients for work while it's in progress or when they have completed it. For ongoing work, they should obtain new financial planning agreements each year to renew the financial planning process.

Some advisors do all their work on a fee-for-service basis instead of commission or advisory account percentage fees. One example would be the financial advisor for an employer-sponsored retirement plan who receives payment on a billing basis. This represents an approach different from the more traditional one involving a percentage fee for the plan's investment assets.

Practitioners can apply the same process for other disciplines of financial services, such as insurance reviews, investment analysis, employer benefit reviews, and all other business lines that they historically have conducted on a commission or percentage-fee-for-assets-under-management basis.

If an employer prefers to cover all the employer-sponsored retirement plan expenses, this billing method provides transparency. It also simplifies the employer's deduction of the plan fees. The employer may prefer that plan participants incur some of the retirement plan's management expenses. This usually involves plan participants who share an ownership in the company. In such a case, advisory fees paid from assets under management would allow that to occur.

The financial advisor should confer with the client to determine the best approach for each service rendered.

Op-Ed

Everyone wants financial planning. But who is willing to pay for it?

Beyond advisory fee–based assets under management through the RIA, a discipline exists for fee-for-service advisory business. This represents the Financial Planning Specialist investing time and effort to offer objective advice and consulting in the client's best interest. A basic package of services would include an individual financial analysis and topics of net worth, cash flow, and retirement planning.

Part of the Financial Planning Specialist's work could include researching select topics for a client and then generating a report of the findings. The Financial Planning Specialist would follow up with a consult to ensure that the client's decision-making process is well-advised.

Advanced topics such as business entity structure, tax planning, estate conservation, and numerous other matters, may require more in-depth financial planning. These cases require collaboration with accountants as well as business and estate attorneys. They potentially can become fertile ground for fee-based financial planning.

In all regards, financial planning represents a methodical process requiring a systematic approach to all aspects of client development and advice delivery. A plethora of detailed processes follow that requires paperwork and documentation. The firm's RIA would need to provide clients with the appropriate forms used in financial planning.

The Financial Planning Specialist must initiate a preliminary discussion with the client concerning the magnitude and scope of the financial planning engagement. They must cover all details involved in implementing the financial plan. The Financial Planning Specialist should coordinate with key advisors to achieve the necessary cohesiveness to assure that the financial plan comes together. The most essential requirement for the Financial Planning Specialist is to identify and confirm the client's willingness to execute the financial planning agreement and commit to the fee payment terms.

None of the other financial services disciplines acquire revenue directly from the client like fee-for-service financial planning. Most of the time, investment advisory accounts assess a percentage fee from assets under management. Insurance and annuity products pay the agent an initial commission—and often renewal commissions—from the financial companies. However, for the most part, the financial planning client pays the financial planning fee directly. This approach requires commitment and intentionality on the part of the client.

Some Financial Planning Specialists, who also serve as part of the investment advisory group, assess investment accounts with a percentage fee that includes a fee for aspects of financial planning. This requires a signed financial planning agreement (initially and each year going forward) indicating that $0 billing occurs through the financial planning agreement.

The firm should disclose the portion of the investment advisory fee allocated to financial planning. They should also confirm this fee with the client in the investment advisory agreement. The advantage to this approach is that fee assessment recurs automatically with no requirement for the client to write a check each month, quarter, or year.

However, the client could perceive this as a conflating of services. Fee-for-services that occur through percentage assessments to investment accounts can confuse clients. And the fee structure can change inadvertently, commensurate with the work performed when accounts are either drawn down, declined, or increased.

The cleanest method involves simply billing the client with an invoice based purely on the work performed for financial planning. This takes strength on the part of the Financial Planning Specialist to command adequate fees on an ongoing basis, and it also takes the right kind of client who favors work performed that way. Clients and practitioners often advocate this model. It offers a sense of greater transparency and a clear fit for the anticipated service the client will receive.

If a collaboration exists among professionals of different disciplines, such as an Accounting Professional, a Legal Professional, and a Financial Planning Professional, each should bill the client separately. The circle of advisors should communicate regarding billing rates and current industry standards and pass this information along to the client.

Some Financial Planning Specialists may consult with tax and legal professionals. These consultants would bill the financial services group for their services. The financial planning engagement invoice should reflect these costs along with the services directly rendered by the Financial Planning Specialist.

In all circumstances, the success of the financial planning work depends on collecting revenues from clients for the services provided. Borrowing from the CPA firm's model—where clients pay for services based on the accountant's time and effort—the financial services practice would need to establish a billing and collections policy.

Some practices may require payment up-front for most, and possibly all, services that they render. Many would require a portion paid up-front, additional payments at certain points of the project, and the balance at the project's completion.

Any of these will depend on the scope and magnitude of the financial planning engagement. These may vary based on whether the practice is offering the service on behalf of a business, an organization, or an individual client. The financial services practice should also take into consideration the client's cash flow when determining the payment schedule, as some entities and individuals receive revenue on a more structured basis.

The practice may complete some financial planning engagements—those limited in scope and magnitude—in a shorter time period with no ongoing engagement or fee structure. They can develop other financial planning agreements annually as they expect them to continue in subsequent years.

When a financial services practice anticipates financial planning to extend for multiple years, they often require the client to pay a greater amount up front as the work they perform in the first year proves more labor-intensive and lays the foundation for subsequent years. In all regards, practices should obtain a signed financial planning agreement each year that clearly communicates goals, tasks, and expectations.

Both the Financial Planning Specialist and the client can experience goodwill through financial planning work. In the end, the delivery of timely and prudent advice enables clients to make sound financial decisions. And it allows the Financial Planning Specialist to complete the project with a clear sense of accomplishment.

The Details

Years ago, when I passed the Certified Financial Planner CFP' board exam, I was looking forward to serving my clients through financial planning. I anticipated the sense of gratification I would experience when I successfully rendered services and various developed planning topics that helped clients gain insight and realize financial gain. I would receive monetary compensation based purely on the merit of the work itself and not on product selection resulting from specific financial services advice.

At least two obstacles prevented me from accomplishing this. First, I was approaching my mid-thirties at the time and still in the early stages of my experiential knowledge of financial planning. Second, the overall consumer mindset back then rarely strayed from the traditional approach to financial services where the client compensates the Financial Professional based on a product transaction of either an investment account or an insurance policy.

With age, experience, and the passage of time, I conducted more conversations about financial planning work. I executed more engagements that culminated in signed financial planning agreements and financial planning work on a fee-for-service basis.

Over the years, net worth, cash flow, and retirement planning charted the course for the individual financial planning market. These represent the core categories that most clients seek to better understand. Client estate planning needs range from basic directives of asset disposition at the time of estate settlement, to more advanced conservation and gift-planning topics.

Closely held businesses—and business continuity and succession—represent the foundational topics that practitioners typically research for business owners, their families, and key personnel. The more in-depth engagements involve business transfer and taxation.

When dealing with estate conservation, Financial Planning Specialists should team up with accountants and attorneys to provide a more holistic financial planning approach. Each participant can showcase the expertise needed to execute the financial plan, and all can gain credibility by utilizing each other's knowledge and experience. Determine the billing based on the level of involvement and each professional's agreed-upon rate.

In each case, the advice offered, and the financial plan developed *are the product.* The attorney and the accountant each obtained an engagement letter for services, and the Financial Planning Specialist obtained the financial planning agreement.

As a Financial Planning Specialist, you can access several platforms for delivering financial services to clients. For instance, you can work with some clients on an à la carte basis. Based on their needs and preferences, these clients will pick and choose from a menu of services. Other clients will require planning that requires ongoing engagement through regularly scheduled meetings and services.

You can also operate financial planning on a retainer basis. This involves an on-demand format based on the client's needs during an agreed-upon time period. In each of these cases, you will establish a financial planning agreement and access fees based on billable time, or on the amount charged for completing the project.

Some clients will display a natural predisposition to the financial planning thought process. They perceive that an agreed-upon, specified guideline to accomplish the goals stated in the planning process represents the best value. They see this as objective advice that doesn't make them feel obligated to do transactional financial services business. But they often *will* conduct business with the firm to implement financial planning priorities. They feel confident conducting this business through the financial services group that provided the financial planning services. Overall, these clients prefer doing business in a manner that allows for what they would deem an added element of independence.

An ensemble model that allows for different specialists, such as an Investment Advisor and an Insurance Agent, can add value to the Financial Planning Specialist's work. Clients will observe a higher level of expertise among the specialists who work alongside other accredited professionals. Each of these practitioners can engage in more advanced discussions in their area of expertise.

The financial services group needs to maintain independence regarding the financial services platforms they use to offer different product and service options. It is usually the case that they will carefully select a few financial companies based on the companies' industry excellence and familiarity with client account service and management. In this way, they communicate to their clients a credibility-building message of independence and broad access.

Though the industry has shifted to some degree toward more fee-for-service work, many clients still demonstrate a reluctance regarding a fee-for-service structure. They may indicate a preference for doing financial services business built around the traditional format. This is where the Financial Professional receives compensation based on needs analysis and the implementation of financial services.

In this context, business culmination results in commissions paid for insurance, annuities, and retail investing of stocks, bonds, and mutual funds for those clients. The respective insurance agencies and broker/dealers generate the commissions for those product sales.

For investment advisory accounts, the RIA assesses advisory fees to accounts based on the advice rendered and not on transactions completed. Even in this context, clients may still require ongoing education on the merits of financial planning. This also provides an extra layer of validation for the accounts that the financial services group has already established for the clients.

An abbreviated financial planning component may exist for clients who primarily seek to establish traditional investment accounts and insurance policies. The financial services group could establish an engagement and financial planning agreement to provide these clients with an objective review of their current assets and budgeting.

Throughout this process, the client's Personal Financial Website allows them to link all of their accounts together for daily updates and reviews. Clients can access various functionalities that enable them to manipulate data, such as retirement dates based on current assumptions.

The website also enables clients to digitally store vital records, such as estate and business documents. Another website feature allows clients to securely store photos of real estate properties and other assets. This proves helpful and saves time when they are required to file a homeowner's insurance claim and need personal property replacement verification.

A Paraplanner Financial Website Concierge champions the management of the Personal Financial Website. In addition to communicating with clients regarding website use, this team member can prove instrumental in gathering and inputting data and generating financial planning reports. The financial services group could employ them as a traditional employee that works on an hourly or salaried basis, or as an independent contractor on an as-needed basis. As the Financial Professional, you would make the decision based on the level of client demand for the service.

If you determine that the concierge's work and assigned duties are in high demand, then assigning them an employee status may prove feasible. If the workflow seems inconsistent, you may not see enough need to justify staff employment. In that situation, if the concierge's schedule appears flexible and autonomous, then consider setting up a contracted labor arrangement. The concierge's role allows the Financial Planning Specialist to focus on relationship building for existing clients and business development for additional financial planning.

Offering fee-based financial planning and fee-for-service work sets your financial services group apart in the industry. Bear in mind that this type of business may or may not represent the highest revenue component of the financial services practice. And the magnitude of business developed may vary for different practitioners. It all hinges on the firm's emphasis, the clients' readiness, the Financial Planning Specialist's skill, and the reach of partnering CPAs and Financial Professionals in promoting the service.

Nevertheless, offering financial planning as a core discipline will enhance your practice's objectivity and respectability. If the industry continues to transition toward fee-based work, you will be a step ahead.

CHAPTER 9

Three Most Important Keys: Communication, Communication, Communication

Considerations for the CPA

As a managing CPA partner, communicate with the Financial Professional your views on developing the practice's financial services division. You might find it beneficial to jot down your thoughts. Complete a first draft and then come back to it later for review. You may choose to revise a few of the statements, but the core of what you value is in there somewhere. Step away from it again for a period. Then revisit it to evaluate what's worth keeping—or possibly adding, as you may have come up with new ideas.

If you work in a multi-partner practice, go over what you have written with your peers and associates to receive their input. Establish some consensus regarding what you would like to incorporate into a business development plan. When you are ready, share this with the Financial Professional. Decide what's negotiable and what's not. Suggest that the Financial Professional develop their own points for reflection and schedule a meeting to integrate ideas toward a workable business model.

Mutual trust represents an essential component of the business relationship. You cultivate this trust as you engage in open and honest dialogue. Communication acts like the oil circulating through a precision machine allowing for optimal performance. When you establish a straightforward platform of sustained communication, you open the way for top-quality business development.

You and the Financial Professional should identify your individual communication preferences, including mode and frequency. Schedule meetings to discuss topics such as business development, revenue generation, client satisfaction, and referrals. Don't merely problem-solve. Take time to celebrate successes as well.

Establish a structure for conflict-resolution and decision-making for all aspects of developing and managing the financial services business. Since the financial services operate as a subsidiary of the CPA firm, it is customary for the CPA to make the final decision regarding business practices. Of course, you should offer proper deference to the Financial Professional's input since the execution of logistics is primarily their responsibility. The Financial Professional brings valuable industry knowledge and business experience to the partnership. Their counsel should carry a great deal of weight as you deliberate the best possible outcome for all parties.

Considerations for the Financial Professional

As the Financial Professional, you and your staff should always conduct yourselves as guests in the CPA firm. This creates a gracious ambiance for the work setting and promotes goodwill throughout the organization.

The Financial Professional will assume the role as a trusted advisor to the CPA. Consider it a privilege and a great responsibility to provide this level of guidance. In this regard, seek out leadership training for yourself and for your management team, accessing the best resources from both inside and outside the industry.

Consistently promote the vision and mission of the financial services group based on the established business model. As a team leader, internalize the key tenets of the strategic partnership and speak freely to both the financial services staff and CPA firm staff regarding goals and objectives.

Strive to maintain an upbeat tone within the organization. Whenever adverse events or moments of conflict occur, initiate resolution through productive discussions with peers and mentors. You will discover that quiet reflection also enables you to return to a place of peace and confidence.

Be yourself, but endeavor to be your *best* self. No one expects perfection, and it is pointless to put on appearances. But choose your words carefully as you endeavor to communicate all aspects of business development and management. It is through shared labor that relationships are forged to build a sustainable strategic partnership.

As the Financial Professional, you should hold regular staff meetings and make the most of the time available. Be sure to encourage your employees and affirm them in their work. Don't wait until their next scheduled evaluation to identify areas where they need to sharpen their skills. Do this as you work alongside them. In this way, you can reinforce improvement as you see it happen. Then, when you do meet with them for their evaluation, you both can enjoy an edifying discussion rather than endure an awkward confrontation.

Schedule an annual meeting with staff members for similar reinforcement purposes. Seek to strike a balance between an authoritative (but not authoritarian) role and one that beckons collegial rapport. Install a metrics system to communicate compensation schedules and possible increases to keep valued personnel properly engaged and motivated.

If you've developed a multidisciplinary practice, you should regularly conduct business development and management meetings for the Financial Professionals. Informally converse with each one to uncover areas requiring skill development and, when needed, to resolve potential conflict. This helps ensure that the production unit fires on all cylinders and contributing members reach their full potential.

Devise a system for reporting business revenue and profits to the CPAs. This keeps the CPAs well-informed and establishes accountability and shared reward. The prospect of success motivates people. Business partnerships thrive when they can attribute their achievements to a mutual effort. Likewise, during stages of development when the practice doesn't meet its production goals, the Financial Professional must communicate the insight needed for improved outcomes.

Enthusiasm and personality can fade over time, but proven systems endure. Successful companies develop procedures they can replicate. Future generations can perpetuate these procedures to allow business to continue beyond any one practitioner's career.

Commentary

The field of financial services is something of a demand business. Still, when creating a practice, the Financial Professional must actively market to secure enough business to sustain viability. This works well for Financial Professionals since they tend to be outgoing and sales oriented.

CPAs hold the advantage of managing a practice that is unquestionably a demand service. Their work is vital for their clients, if for no other reason than keeping them in compliance with federal and state tax laws. If violated, infractions can result in penalties, fines, or even incarceration. However, CPAs should also orient themselves toward ongoing business development.

Both Financial Professionals and CPAs should exhibit the highest level of skill in rendering their services. But even the best practitioners can't build a thriving client base without promoting their business. When it comes to communicating the mission statement of the CPA and the Financial Professional's partnership, everyone in the firm should assume an active role.

To accomplish this, partners and team members should consider memberships in local civic, social, and nonprofit organizations. These offer time-honored platforms for networking. Sometimes the relationships developed from these affiliations produce business directly. Often, they simply serve to build camaraderie and help your firm establish a trustworthy image in the business community as you form core alliances.

Marketing campaigns, such as community fundraiser sponsorships, also provide advertising and exposure. Many leading accounting and financial services practices participate in these activities. But if that defines the extent of your business development initiatives, the tenor of the partnership's business activity could be good…but not robust.

The partnership's greatest business development potential lies in the nearly limitless opportunities generated by client introductions. With the mutual referrals available through local professional alliances, you can exponentially multiply your community presence to create a self-sustaining and perpetually-promoting ecosystem of services.

Financial Professionals refer clients for accounting services, while CPAs refer clients for financial services. This only works when all parties equitably experience the rewards established through that collaborative effort. CPAs reap a great reward when they witness a skillfully executed estate plan providing their client with tax savings through the right financial services products. The Financial Professional feels equally satisfied to observe clients finding tax savings and avoiding unnecessary hardship resulting from timely and well-delivered accounting and tax planning services.

However, without compensation, many of those successes would never occur. Everyone wants payment for their time and effort. The business developed among licensed professionals produces shared revenue. Business instituted between equity owners realizes an increase in business value. All possess common goals that transform perfunctory involvement into enthusiastic participation.

We would all like to think that we would go the extra mile to help a client by connecting with professionals of varying disciplines. To some extent, we do take those measures based on our level of dedication and commitment. But what enhances the practitioner's level of alacrity and persistence is the potential for compensation in a profitable strategic partnership context.

It's essential that you maintain contact with these professional alliances, whether through email, telephone conversations, or in-person meetings. Ensure that the content comes across as both informative and congenial. We most readily do the things we enjoy. When we make the process enjoyable, people are more likely to participate.

CPAs like to know that the Financial Professional has created a positive experience for their client referrals. They value receiving updates from the Financial Professional assuring them that these clients are being systematically cared for. They shouldn't have to seek out the Financial Professional for these updates, and they should never hear about client dissatisfaction directly from the client. Likewise, Financial Professionals appreciate knowing that the clients they referred are pleased with the tax and accounting services and that they maintain a high regard for the CPA.

When a client provides negative feedback, the team of professionals should provide clear communication and work together to rectify the matter to the client's satisfaction. Demonstrate a "whatever-it-takes" mentality to strive for best practices.

Ongoing improvement comprises a vital part of business services and requires a commitment from all participants. When a client's account requires correction, complete this according to the firm's policies and procedures in compliance with industry and regulatory guidelines.

For broker/dealer business, communicate with the OSJ to ensure that the measures put forth follow all requirements. For accounting business, follow industry protocol to address those issues as well.

When you successfully address a client's needs and concerns, you conserve business and strengthen relationships. Use it as an opportunity to reinforce that your practice operates with integrity and in its clients' best interest. All parties can then learn and work together to strengthen the client–professional relationship for the future.

Skilled communication is essential to producing optimal internal rapport among your practitioners and staff, especially when it comes to recognizing their accomplishments. Offering proper recognition for a team member's achievement produces immeasurable goodwill.

When you observe that an employee needs to improve in a certain area, first consider their personality type and how they respond to feedback. Approach them accordingly with genuine affirmation and a sincere commitment to assist them toward improvement. The best coaching occurs during regular day-to-day conversation where the staff member doesn't interpret it as highly corrective or confrontational. It should flow from an established office culture where all participants—including the leaders—pursue excellence on an ongoing basis.

No one can achieve perfection. But if you work toward providing the highest quality service possible, it can result in mutual reward. The organization's well-being depends on staff incentive programs with systematic and observable measurements. Enhanced production brings enhanced compensation. Keep salaried and hourly staff informed as to how they can earn merit-based compensation increases.

Any well-run organization should operate on the premise that employees must demonstrate quality work and dedication. Hiring the right people and rewarding them for their efforts represents a foundational principle of competent leadership.

Each year, all employees should receive compensation based on a standard cost-of-living increase. Reward the next tier of compensation to those staff members who show initiative by improving an aspect of the operation's efficiency or profitability. This could include identifying cost-saving measures or uncovering new opportunities that lead to business development. Taking this type of initiative creates a "buy-in" mindset among all team members. It emphasizes that they work *with* the firm and not just *for* it.

Most importantly, a simple, well-timed "thank you" and heartfelt recognition among the peer group costs little financially but pays big dividends.

Op-Ed

Talk is cheap. Not talking is expensive.

When an employee express dissatisfaction with their work environment, it is often a matter of communication. More specifically, it's a *lack* of communication.

Even more specifically, it's a lack of *quality* communication.

This can be said for partners and clients, too. Some organizations operate on a "need to know" basis. They may use this approach because of the sensitive nature of the information and a concern for misperception. But this can breed mistrust among participants who feel that they are "kept in the dark."

Other organizations deliver general information as they correspond through memos and emails. This type of surface communication may not adequately relay the vision and inclusion needed to engage the recipients. When this occurs, employees, partners, and clients alike could feel like they are merely an account number or a name on a file.

The most successful organizations consistently provide a cogent message of direction, involvement, and appreciation. Even when you're offering coaching points to a staff member, make sure that you clearly communicate your intent to take something good and make it even better. Individual employees can then acknowledge areas for growth and share a vested stake in making the whole team stronger.

Each staff member should feel that the financial services group leadership keeps their best interests in mind. Field, address, and even solicit staff members' questions. This will draw out existing concerns in the early stages where you can manage them more easily. And leaders must readily admit that they themselves are imperfect as well. This presents the leadership team as being both reasonable and approachable.

Turnover of quality personnel costs money and disrupts the business flow. Keeping staff members maintains revenue for the firm. Carve out small blocks of time throughout the year to dialogue with individual staff members. This could provide an "ounce of prevention" to avoid the need for "a pound of cure."

Partner disputes can also arise from a lack of communication. When this occurs, it's often because they have allowed tensions to fester instead of seeking resolution through a healthy exchange of their thoughts and feelings. It is easy to let the demands of a busy schedule get in the way of taking time for productive discussion. Be sure to prioritize the time required to create a platform for both formal and informal communication.

Just as a simple thank-you pays big dividends with team members, the same applies to clients. There is no substitute for the support team practicing basic courtesies, such as a pleasant tone of voice over the phone. These simple acts demonstrate that the firm recognizes that the client is important and, ultimately, is the reason the firm exists.

A client's dissatisfaction may peak with a disagreement over a service issue, but it may well have begun as a smaller matter that could have been resolved if detected sooner. Keeping clients maintains revenue for the firm; losing clients costs money. Proactive communication is essential.

The Details

Communication occurs in many ways. We typically convey formal information in writing, while we engage in casual exchanges in person or over the phone. We generate nonverbal communication based on what we do and don't do. All in all, we're sending and receiving messages during most of our waking hours.

The main point regarding communication within the CPA financial services partnership is that it should happen on a consistent basis. Partners should establish scheduled rotations for meetings about partner earnings, firmwide compliance, and vision-casting. You can conduct these either on location, online, or by conference call. Generate reports that further detail goal identification and realization. Don't neglect informal conversations, as these reinforce relationships and foster enjoyment in co-laboring.

Not doing these things also portrays a type of communication, and it's not a positive one. It sends a message that other priorities distract from building a thriving financial services partnership. Worse, it could depict a lack of organization or profitability.

Financial Professionals should get to know staff members and speak with each one regularly. This builds an element of camaraderie within the group. A steady flow of communication with emails, messaging, phone calls, and in-person conversations represents the benchmark of a healthy organization.

When turnover occurs, it's possible that the employee was pursuing superior compensation or promotion elsewhere. Many times, it happens because the leadership failed to create an inclusive atmosphere. Therefore, show a genuine interest in each staff member's well-being regardless of rank or tenure.

Since not all communication is written or verbal, it is up to the financial services group's leadership to be sensitive to each employee's nonverbal communication expressed through behavior and conduct. An otherwise productive employee may suddenly become disorganized and unfocused. This may or may not have anything to do with the work environment. The employee may not feel comfortable talking about the issue. However, the leadership can encourage them by showing extra care and attentiveness, even if it doesn't specifically relate to the matter itself.

Employees appreciate a work environment where the leadership doesn't appear aloof or disingenuous when it comes to being a fellow team member. It is embedded deep within the human psyche for all of us to have a "place at the table." So, a sense of unity can provide a quality of involvement transcending compensation issues. Of course, it goes without saying that the firm should maintain market rates of financial compensation. But emotional compensation built on good rapport can also provide a bonus to recruit and retain the right people.

The end goal of client communication is more communication. Clients can't have too much supportive communication, especially when it comes to scheduled meeting confirmations, and new business follow-ups. Clients will welcome systematic, specific correspondence and regard it as attentive and informative.

However, it is possible to "drip" on them too much by excessive emails and marketing blasts. An example of this would be when you initiate a client business development campaign to promote a specific financial services topic, such as financial planning. You should measure and conduct this type of effort to allow for manageable follow-up. The staff should only send a reasonable number of emails at any one interval. That way, clients don't feel bombarded, and the financial services group contact person can complete the campaign in a timely and efficient manner.

On the other hand, distributing quarterly newsletters from an asset manager serves as a reminder that the firm is still conducting business on clients' behalf. Clients may never read them, but it's an indicator that the practice remains in good standing.

The most effective client communication happens one-on-one between clients and the financial services team members. It begins with the referring CPA acting as the most trusted advisor regarding tax and accounting, and the Financial Professional directing client financial services meetings and correspondence as a most trusted advisor as well.

The financial services support personnel play an equally important role. Systematic outreach from the Client Experience Specialist affirms the value the firm places on each client. Administrative Assistants demonstrate client appreciation by maintaining client data for account distributions, address changes, death claims, and a wide variety of other services rendered throughout the year. These efforts go a long way toward client retention and account conservation, particularly during times of economic uncertainty.

Interaction with the financial companies with which your firm is affiliated composes another vital circle of communication. If you work within a larger CPA firm or group of companies, a corporate office structure may exist beyond the local financial services group. In this case, it is essential that you not only maintain cordial relationships with the local team of professionals but with the corporate office team members as well.

The corporate office may employ individuals dedicated to supporting a particular financial discipline, such as investments, insurance, retirement plans, annuities, or financial planning. Specialists at the local level should regularly correspond with these contacts. If senior leadership at the corporate office provides oversight for your organization's operations, compliance, and profitability, strive to maintain a cordial working relationship with them.

Often, the vision of the central office doesn't exactly mirror that of the local office. When this is the case, leadership should promote free expression characterized by a mutual respect for differing viewpoints— and affirmation of all involved. These exchanges should always result in a more vital collaboration toward a unified mission statement.

Relationships with investment companies, insurance companies, and vendors also thrive on communication. Specialists from the financial services group should maintain a positive rapport with the financial companies' key contact personnel through which business is conducted. This includes new business proposals and product-knowledge marketing contacts, and the personnel that provides help with client account management and service.

When you cover service points, make notes for the client files. This helps assure quality service when, in particular, you identify the most knowledgeable and helpful financial company personnel. Prioritize communication with those individuals. Financial companies perceive members of the financial services group as clients and strive for optimal customer satisfaction. Staff members from the financial services group should express their appreciation to vendors and financial service companies for their assistance.

It all starts and stops with effective communication. In the end, all the participants—CPAs, staff, financial services clients, and company representatives—are clients. Participants demonstrate care for other participants to ensure that the entire ecosystem remains healthy and thriving.

It bears repeating that the financial services group is there by invitation from the CPA firm. Therefore, if you must ration communication—like time, energy, and other resources—direct the most concentrated effort to the CPA firm. The bonds between the accounting firm and the financial services group support all the other relationships. If that relationship remains vibrant, it will set the tone for the entire organization. In other words, when Financial Professionals and CPAs practice effective communication, it pays off. Handsomely.

CHAPTER 10

Managing Seasons of Change

Considerations for the CPA

Change happens constantly. Change resulting from a team member's departure can disrupt business development and production. The CPA firm must devise a contingency plan if one of its support staff members resigns or becomes incapacitated. The same applies to the Financial Professional and their support staff.

The key to weathering such a change is to put a business model in place where the components are *interchangeable*.

Cross-training your staff increases your capacity to seamlessly weather staff turnover. If an employee cannot execute their primary tasks, other team members can step in to ensure that client service continues with minimal interruption. In some cases, you may find it necessary to recruit outside talent to fulfill the team member's role.

When the change involves the retirement of a partner or key practitioner, having a replicable business development and management system in place will prove invaluable. Businesses earn their appraisal value in part based on their continuity and reliability. If a business' client sustainability depends on one individual, it reduces long-term viability and decreases the value overall.

When a partner or key practitioner leaves on negative terms or to start their own practice, make client retention a top priority. A change of this magnitude requires that you swiftly initiate client communication. If needed, increase your support staff to successfully sustain ongoing account management. A merger with peer firms or groups could represent another option.

A noncompete agreement should be in place to bolster client retention. All participants should clearly communicate regarding the nature and enforcement of this agreement. Within the partnership and supportive professionals—such as the firm's legal counsel—a working understanding should exist regarding the agreement's execution and the business continuation plan.

As you focus on contingency planning, seek legal counsel to gain clarity and vision. As ideas come to mind, share these with your attorney. Don't wait until difficulties arise to seek solutions. It may be too late at that time to implement them successfully.

Trust your instincts regarding how to prepare for other adverse circumstances that require change. For example, if a natural disaster took place, which team members would you deem as mission-critical?

In such cases, retain personnel who can successfully operate in a limited capacity with reduced resources.

Beyond planning for in-house and local disruptions, you must anticipate change on the political and economic stage as well. If the government passes sweeping legislation that affects the way you conduct business, you must strategize regarding how to comply and remain current. For example, if industry regulations altered how the financial services business generates fees or commissions, you would need to research all your options.

Regulatory organizations that influence and determine licensing requirements and disclosure can also mandate change. This could cause the financial services business to resemble traditional accounting work more closely, emphasizing fee-for-service engagements with compensation based more on time or a project-billing basis. This would replace fee-based percentage for assets under management or commission based on products or services. Industry-wide alteration of this type could require you to overhaul both your business structure and personnel requirements.

Economic cycles impact all aspects of business, including financial services. During times of contraction, you should escalate client services to conserve relationships and account values. You may find yourself exerting more effort only to sustain even less business development and revenue. Minimize financial leverage when these cycles occur. This reduces business risk, helps you to maintain a welcoming business environment and prevents undue pressure.

Trying times can produce strategic shifts. Industry competitors may experience changes resulting in mergers and acquisitions. Maintain ongoing conversations with peer firms and associates to help uncover lucrative opportunities.

Considerations for the Financial Professional

As a Financial Professional, make business contingency planning for the CPA firm and the financial services practice central to your thinking. You should analyze all aspects of risk management. Establish personal disability insurance and business-overhead disability insurance in the event that a key participant becomes incapacitated and the firm loses productivity.

You would also need to plan for the loss of life. Implement the insurance coverage required to replace the economic benefit of any participant whose death precipitates business disruption. Make sure that a buy-sell agreement is in place. This would permit business continuation for the practice and settlement for the deceased business partner's estate. This would ensure that all parties would be made whole in the resulting ownership transition for the financial services practice.

The Financial Professional should anticipate and plan for personnel turnover. Cross-train your employees so that they can carry out essential support duties with minimal disruption.

If team members engage in disputes over personnel departure, clients could suffer confusion and dismay, and all parties could fare worse as a result. Ill will in such matters can jeopardize valuable relationships. Maintain a strict adherence to the firm's established contract agreements to maintain integrity and avoid discord within the firm.

Since the Financial Professionals develop business jointly, they become familiar with each client's account. This allows for optimal business continuation if any of the team members incur a setback. Maintain connections with peers outside the firm to create an open door for recruiting additional Financial Professionals if the need arises.

As a Financial Professional, you are in the business of following economic and current events. You should expect to provide leadership and counsel to the CPAs regarding business management trends.

If you anticipate new expenses or revenue loss, develop a plan and share it with the partners. If it includes a key staffing change, obtain a consensus among the firm leadership to ensure the best outcome. Decisively and promptly revise any financial forecasting to guide the practice activities in the right direction.

We often resist change, but change happens all the same. Some changes may prove temporary, and some permanent. Responding to change in the right way produces the best results over time.

For times of economic downturn, you may be required to exert extra effort to strengthen and sustain existing client relationships and conserve account values. In other words, short-term pain could foster long-term gain.

If you experience a season that interrupts business as usual, you may benefit from shifting assignments among support staff. In the same way that a manufacturing plant may be converted for other uses during wartime, the roles of support team members may change. Flexibility will prove essential.

Under normal circumstances, a Registered Sales Assistant focuses on executing routine client trade orders, basic account summaries, and note preparations for client review meetings. During times of upheaval, their primary focus may shift to account reviews that emphasize timely and strategic changes driven by market and economic disruption.

Support personnel, including Registered Sales Assistants, should practice proactive client communication during seasons of economic uncertainty. This goes a long way in conveying a message of care, attentiveness, and reassurance. Communicate with CPA partners the need to increase their client outreach initiatives as well.

The most valuable resource and lifeblood of both the CPA practice and the financial services practice is the client's well-being and their satisfaction in the client experience.

Commentary

Significant changes affecting the partnership can occur outside of the natural cycle of development. The CPA firm may merge with another, or the financial group may materially shift because of a change of broker/dealer, RIA, or general insurance agency. Changes within the organization may also occur, such as partners parting ways. Adapt by moving along with the changes.

Change that occurs quickly requires a quick response. As the CPA and Financial Professional senior leadership, you should discuss the practice's continuity. Contact business attorneys for input on decisions regarding business operations. Include staff members in the discussion as soon as you determine it is feasible and permissible. The partners should agree on how to conduct client communication. Convey a well-worded, consistent message to those whom the change will impact.

Some partners may want to sell out to successor partners, or a consensus may exist to maintain practices individually while continuing separate partnerships between accounting and financial services firms. The long-term outcomes can vary.

Practitioners can attempt to maintain existing partnerships through a different structure; but all too often, partnerships cease. When this occurs, reference the business agreements established at the strategic partnership's inception for guidance in protocol and procedure. Make every effort to serve all parties' interests in the most beneficial manner.

If the magnitude of services diminishes, it may reduce the need for specific support positions. For example, you may no longer require the role of some Financial Professional Specialists if fewer Financial Professionals can cover a wider variety of services. Aspects of the practice could begin to resemble the initial stages before the scale and volume of business increased through the various seasons of growth. When changes occur that require a modification of personnel and support staff, generate communication in a manner that is clear but sensitive.

If you are able to sustain a significant volume of business, you could return to higher profit margins with lower magnitude as in the initial stages of development. In this regard, the business comes full circle for both financial and accounting services. It may exist on a smaller scale with fewer participants but would continue, nonetheless.

Op-Ed

Change is constant. Anticipate change.

You will invest a great deal of effort into creating and advancing the business model. As a result, it's natural that you would want to prolong the life cycle of the business.

Sustained production marks the early seasons of the practice. You cultivate activity, generate referrals, and conduct business. However, seasons change, and so can the complexion of the financial services partnership.

As time goes on, the abundance of fresh, new leads generated by the partners may give way to referrals accessed from established clients. The

90:10 ratio of partner referrals to self-initiated referrals may, instead, become 10:90 partner referrals to self-initiated referrals. Anticipate a cycle of this sort. Over time, the practice matures, and the volume of partner referrals reduces because you have already contacted the bulk of the CPA firm client base.

Either way, the key to success lies in generating a high number of client meetings and phone calls each week. The activity pipeline must stay full. Some referring partners create more business development than others, and this can increase or decrease as time goes on. Partners who did not show support initially may show more support as they become increasingly aware of the business model's success and client satisfaction rate. And nothing beats quality, reciprocal referrals from specialists of different disciplines within the strategic partnership.

Anticipate additional changes. For example, a partner you relied upon for business development may retire or leave the firm, thus disrupting the existing client referral stream. This reinforces the importance of multiple partner client referral arrangements.

If clients have experienced less-than-optimal results because of a recessed economy or lackluster investment market, the departure of a key figure in the firm may prompt them to pursue perceived "greener pastures" elsewhere. The best approach to keeping clients through good times and bad begins with informative and honest communication. We naturally tend to avoid potentially difficult conversations when account values decline, but remaining consistent in client outreach and dialogue will greatly enhance sustainability.

If partners leave the practice on positive terms, they often continue as clients themselves and remain important centers of influence for the clients they referred. As a result, these clients continue to maintain their accounts.

However, the departure of the referring partner can negatively affect client relationships over time. When this happens, clients with accounts at multiple firms become vulnerable, especially if they established an advisor relationship before doing business with your group. A competing firm may entice these clients by offering a "breakpoint reduction" in fees to consolidate accounts and move them to a firm where a prior allegiance still exists.

When a partner exits because of a disagreement or division, this could adversely affect your ongoing client relationships with their referrals. Those loyal to the referring partner may close or move their accounts if they perceive the partner received unfair treatment. If perceived or actual impropriety occurred on the part of the partner, that, too, can result in lost accounts. Based on a client's perception of the events that transpired, they may or may not continue to do business.

Partners who become unsupportive of the practice after their departure may exert negative influence over client perceptions. This can result in still more lost accounts. However, if the servicing professional has built strong client relationships, a good chance exists for the practice to sustain the client relationships. And clients may eventually develop a greater rapport with the servicing financial practitioner than the referring partner.

Some former partners may still support the servicing Financial Professional, even if they don't advocate the overall partnership firmwide. It is imperative to maintain constructive relationships among these and all partners. Make it a practice to reach out and demonstrate receptiveness and goodwill, particularly for those partners who may not currently exhibit inclusiveness. Over time, this could produce positive change and result in a profitable relationship.

Show respect for a former or departing partner when their name arises during discussions with other partners and clients. You may lack clarity regarding the details surrounding the departure, so give that partner the benefit of the doubt. Reach an agreement among the remaining partners about what to—and what not to—communicate to clients and outside parties. If the departure negatively affected clients, make every effort to address their concerns and reinforce relationships. Strive for a balance of clarity and tact. Address matters clearly and candidly, avoiding embellishment and bias.

Changes can happen in-house, but they can also originate from outside sources. The same industry regulations that first allowed you to conduct the financial services business within a CPA firm may change to no longer permit that. Administration changes in the financial services industry, government, and professional associations could modify how you conduct business. These agencies could alter policies and procedures restrictions and introduce new licensing requirements. More stringent recordkeeping or service standards could increase staffing and technology needs resulting in higher expenses and lower profitability.

New industry regulations and requirements that affect the CPAs' and Financial Professionals' strategic partnership can create division among the participants. Partners who have accommodated the ups and downs will often maintain their support. Partners who resisted the partnership's establishment may use the changes as opportunities to express concern. Alliances often form within the partnership structure among subgroups. Partnership dynamics surface at points of change, revealing the foundational dispositions and varying viewpoints of different individuals.

Discussions that the partners conducted before establishing the partnership may come to light. Exercise forbearance when partners express varying viewpoints. As communication produces new understanding, perspectives may shift over time. Since business involves the pursuit of profit, money always remains in focus. And when it comes to money, contention can quickly arise.

Following the procedures for best practices enables the partnership to weather challenging transitions and experience a positive outcome. When participants stay together based on a commitment to work things out, and not merely because of imposed protocol, an exceptional outcome can result.

Difficulties turn up the heat and expose our weaknesses. The good news is that difficulties can also bring out the best in us when we are willing to rise to the occasion and learn in the process. In this way, challenging seasons can produce defining moments that forge partnerships to reach their full potential. Seek outside counsel during these times to help lead the partnership down the best path. A legal professional can offer guidance and advice to help partnerships stay together and continue to pursue a common goal.

When points of contention develop among CPAs, the Financial Professionals don't always need to get involved. If the CPAs can settle it between themselves, business can continue without interruption. The same can be said for the Financial Professionals. Often a support structure exists within the financial services company to help resolve conflict. When the larger peer group can work through their own issues, again, business can continue without interruption.

If the partners fail to reconcile a matter, they should work toward an alternative business continuation plan following the guidelines for entity dissolution. Partners may part ways, and CPAs may go in different directions.

Financial Professionals should strive to maintain ongoing relationships with various participants. Ideally, partners would continue to co-labor, but perhaps in a different context with a different affiliation. This, too, will depend on how strongly the participants developed their relationships over time.

If Financial Professionals no longer work together, CPAs should strive to continue conducting business with each one individually, maintaining strong client relationships with the least amount of division. Clients may remain loyal to the practitioner with whom they first established services. Practitioners must work toward conserving client relationships in the best way possible.

If a change occurs to the CPA firm through an outside firm merger or acquisition, the CPAs should exercise sensitivity toward the Financial Professionals. If the change occurs with the financial services group, the Financial Professionals should extend similar consideration to the CPAs. Once you see clearly that change is imminent, initiate clear communication to promote goodwill and understanding. Be honest as you point out the advantages and disadvantages of these potential changes.

A pivotal point to consider would be whether the financial services partnership would continue as the same entity. The acquiring CPA firm may choose not to offer financial services. Or they may work with a different broker/dealer, RIA, or insurance agency. If that's the case, it could require a substantial amount of change to existing accounts and create adversity and alienation for current financial service company affiliations, including securities broker/dealers.

The financial companies with which the partnership was formerly affiliated often will seek to restrict the financial services group from continuing to work with existing clients, creating ongoing contention.

Leadership from these companies may assign current client accounts to their financial representatives. These representatives may initiate communication with those clients about changes in account relationships. This can cause clients to become confused and concerned regarding the Financial Professional's transition. When this occurs, the firm will need to reference existing noncompete agreements. If needed, seek legal counsel for guidance on how best to navigate working with different financial companies.

These competing service company financial representatives often persuade the clients assigned to them at the point of transition to remain with them. Unfortunately, this results in additional business loss.

Like the CPA firm acquisition, the financial services company may also change or combine with another organization. This often results in substantial clerical and administrative work as client accounts are repapered and reestablished, which can significantly disrupt the activity and revenue of the practice.

The tenor and nature of the financial services practice may change based on the proposed new affiliation's culture. The practice partners may not approve of the modifications. After thorough deliberation, they may consider the proposed changes as untenable or undesirable. This decision should take place in advance of the proposed change. You would find it unpleasant and costly to transition along with the current financial company only to go through the process all over again.

When Financial Professionals within the CPA firm become divided or part ways, it evolves somewhat differently than when CPAs separate from the CPA firm. If the CPA firm owns the financial services group, the client accounts belong to the CPA firm. This assumes that the partners built the financial services practice on an independent platform where the broker/dealer could not claim that the accounts belong to them. If the firm is working with an outside broker/dealer, RIA, or independent general insurance agency, issues of noncompete agreements could exist. It is essential that you understand who owns the clients.

When a Financial Professional leaves the practice, those who remain would follow the Operating Agreement and Articles of Organization protocol and continue to work with the departing professional's clients. If the CPA partners referred most of these clients, these CPAs should remain as the primary source for client communication.

However, the departing Financial Professional may seek to take clients with them as they transition to other financial services arrangements. Even those that the CPA firm acquired may express strong preferences for account management assignments. They may ultimately transition with the Financial Professional irrespective of company policy.

When this happens, allow clients directly developed by the departing Financial Professional to transition with that practitioner. You would regret it if the personnel transition caused anyone to contest how you manage client account services and relationships. When situations arise that require legal counsel, pursue the least adversarial resolution.

Any major transition that occurs during an economic downturn adds a level of difficulty to client communication and follow-through. All partnership participants must consistently reassure clients in order to ensure maximum retention and account conservation.

Change is inevitable. You can't avoid change that is based on industry and seasonal adjustments. However, you should give ample deliberation to voluntary or self-initiated change before setting it in motion. Even positive change comes with a price tag. Develop a thorough understanding of whether the changes you are considering are truly worth it.

If the changes you propose emerge from a perceived financial necessity or possible improvement, take the time to consider all possible solutions. Most of the time, we never fully anticipate the costs of change—both materially and nonmaterially. We grossly underestimate the depletion of time, energy, and money. More importantly, relationships developed for years suffer disruption from the day-to-day camaraderie that once provided the heartbeat for the organization. We rarely foresee these unintended outcomes.

When the firm determines that a change represents the best interest of the practice, make the decision and execute the plan without regret and recapitulation.

There is no way for you to correctly assess all the ramifications of change, so the best thing to do is commit and follow through. Don't look back—duplicity of mind only produces an unnecessary distraction from current achievement.

The Details

When the game changes, the game changes—you have no choice but to deal with it. Your initial model of licensed CPAs making regular referrals for direct compensation could change. Industry regulations could change. The most significant change would be if the CPA firm merges with another CPA firm and eliminates the financial services entity. If that occurs, you must find a new way to do business.

Seek to continue as a part of the CPA firm, if possible, as it could provide you with a competitive advantage. CPA firms offer valuable resources and services for a wide range of client needs. You earn credibility from your association with knowledgeable and talented professionals who continue to demonstrate the highest levels of intellectual capital and integrity in client service.

If you remain as a portfolio company of the CPA firm (where CPAs are not securities or insurance licensed), the financial services group can generate revenue for the parent company as a profitable component of EBITDA for the firm.

The CPA firm's financial services partnership structure would establish unitholder value for each partner's stake in the financial services group in determining each partner's realized payout at retirement. This would occur when units in the LLC ownership are tendered in the future. Partners receive compensation in retirement based on the valuation of their shared ownership interest.

If the CPA firm changes, and a place for the financial services business no longer exists, you must adapt. The Financial Professionals could execute a client base buyout from the CPA firm so that divestiture occurs, and the financial services firm would stand on its own.

When this type of epic change occurs for the business model, identify positive outcomes and resolve to pursue business in new ways. You must view the client base's full development as top priority. Drive business deeper from established relationships. In the beginning, your ambition was to go wide to develop your book of business. Having achieved that, you may need to build on those results to develop business at new levels. You should concentrate on working with existing clients to cultivate additional business and client referrals.

You have acquired referrals in the past primarily by observing client relationship circles and requesting introductions. Another unimposing prompt would involve your simply asking your clients to tell their friends, coworkers, and family about the financial services group. When a name comes up as a potential referral, obtain permission from the client both to reach out to the prospect and to obtain their contact information.

Before contacting the prospective referral, ask the client to mention to them that the financial services group will contact them soon. You would then call the prospective client, identify the referral source, and offer your availability to help with any of their financial service needs. Be sure to thank the referral source and update them regarding the eventual outcome. Follow this same process when you provide a referral to a CPA or another professional service provider.

Refer clients to professionals with whom you seek to network. A three-way introductory phone call is often effective once the client identifies the need for a particular service. Briefly cover essential discussion points and establish rapport with the client and the professional service provider.

I will often ask our Client Experience Specialist to schedule a meeting for the client with a professional service provider, such as an estate attorney. If time permits, I will attend that meeting to assist with the discussion and cover vital information. I want to support the professional service provider's efforts to help fulfill the client's needs. This establishes camaraderie and can develop further referrals and new business.

When a partner retires, assume a supportive role before, during, and after the transition. Likely, you can conduct business on their behalf, such as an employer-sponsored retirement plan rollover to an individual retirement account. Insurance needs, such as health, Medicare supplement, long-term care, or life insurance, may also be in order. Use this as an opportunity to demonstrate benevolence and sincere appreciation. Make sure the partner has taken the steps to financially prepare for retirement. Address the needs of the spouse, children, and extended family members as well.

If the retiring partner has served as a center of influence providing client referrals over the years, they will view it as a kind gesture if you provide ongoing feedback indicating that these clients continue to receive quality care. Even when CPAs retire, their clients often stay in touch with their most trusted advisor. Therefore, it is essential that you maintain a good rapport. Retired CPAs can continue to serve as valuable centers of influence for associates who participate in their shared hobbies and activities.

When partners exit for reasons other than retirement, such as moving to another firm, those partners may continue as centers of influence if no competing financial services are in place at their new firm. They could introduce you to their new work associates who can also become clients and provide referrals. These new CPAs may require your services individually or on behalf of their firm for employee benefits, such as retirement plans and insurance services.

When partners part ways on unfavorable terms, attempt to maintain a good standing with them individually, even if they feel less than amicable toward the firm overall. It is a delicate balance to strike, but it is possible to maintain favor with them and retain accounts that they—and their referred clients—have established with you.

Even if the level of contention under which they departed is too great to overcome, extend amity all the same. In this way, they can think well of you even if they don't think well of your firm. Mutual clients within your shared network can be affirmed for your services with minimal disruption or loss of client accounts.

When associate Financial Professionals retire, extend the same courtesies to them as the retiring CPA. When Financial Professionals change firms, some of the shared clients would likely transition with them.

Communicate understanding and offer to maintain services for those clients who find themselves caught in the middle.

When you clearly discern that client loyalties lie with the departing Financial Professional, wish them well and thank them for the opportunity to work with them. Affirm your willingness to serve them in the future if things change.

Avoid contention with departing clients and associate Financial Professionals whenever possible. If disputes escalate and legal counsel becomes involved, follow the counsel's advice, and don't risk violating rules, guidelines, and laws that could prove costly down the road. Life is too short, and time is too precious to waste by becoming embroiled in litigation or overtaken by ill will and negative energy. Furthermore, it can distract you from providing quality client care and developing ongoing business. The opportunity cost of missing out on quality of life and the abundance of new possibilities would be tragic.

When sickness or other hardships affect you or your staff, allow for interruptions and have a contingency plan in place. Cross-training your support staff and Associate Financial Professionals will prove essential. You cannot anticipate every potential setback that could befall your organization. But when setbacks do occur, your firm will greatly benefit if you have trained your staff to efficiently cover their coworkers' assignments.

If one of the associate Financial Professionals experiences a disruption, provide clear communication and ongoing care for their clients. Another associate Financial Professional should service those accounts. Give it your best shot as you attempt to gauge the time scope for this disruption. This will help you allocate the necessary resources required for coverage.

Make arrangements for the affected employee. Consider extended benefits during their leave of absence. Promptly communicate with human resources personnel. Prioritize ongoing contact with the employee and their family. When coworkers inquire about the employee's status, use discretion as you provide updates.

If the time frame becomes extended, or possibly permanent, consider hiring additional personnel to either support the service areas that could become overextended, or the practice discipline directly affected by the disruption.

If regulations change how you conduct business, you must modify your business model. In some parts of the world, regulations have already changed and no longer allow commissions for financial services products sold or advisory fees for investment assets under management. In this context, financial services professionals would only receive compensation for advice given for the work rendered on a fee-for-service basis. If your practice already offers this, you hold a distinct competitive advantage over firms that have not made this service available or prioritized this part of the financial services business.

Providing fee-based financial planning represents a viable service unto itself regardless of industry change. Client preferences are trending toward this format of financial services work. If regulation changes revolutionize industry standards to dictate fee-for-service only, the Financial Planning Specialist would move into a distinctively leading role for the practice. This would, indeed, level the playing field as never before.

If this takes place, you will need to embrace it as you would any other industry modification. Allocate resources to bolster fee-based planning efforts to maintain viability and thrive in this new environment. Financial services may continue with little modification, but compensation and client fee assessment would radically change. Clients would require reeducation. You may find it necessary to facilitate promotional activities to explain how your firm would render services going forward.

None of these details may apply to your practice. But if they ever do, being as prepared as possible will help you maintain a thriving client base and a satisfying financial services career.

CHAPTER 11

Understanding the Cycles of the CPA Firm Financial Services Business

Considerations for the CPA

One way to describe the cycles of a CPA practice's financial services business is to compare them to the four seasons in nature.

First, spring arrives. This is when, as a CPA, you birth the idea of establishing the practice's financial services component. You possess vision and optimism for this strategic partnership to effectively leverage time and revenue beyond the traditional accounting firm format.

Within that traditional format, your staff may maximize their time and energy during peak tax seasons or stretches of increased audit work. Financial services offer an alternative model that isn't based on the finite commodity of time. The Financial Professional serves as an extension of these resources to reach clients and develop business with recurring fees and commissions that build cash flow throughout the year.

As in nature, summer follows spring in the business cycle. Business starts to build and compound. Activity increases for establishing accounting clients, and you find yourself cultivating referrals for financial services clients. A multiplier effect takes hold that often requires additional staffing and resources to reach the next level.

Autumn occurs when you have already reached many of the original prospective clients. At this juncture, you may consider bringing in additional Financial Professional Specialists to develop each client's business potential more fully. For example, if you have emphasized investment asset management, you could now focus on insurance risk management. Or you could give attention to financial planning that would warrant adding a Financial Planning Specialist.

You could include at least one more core component of the ensemble team: a specialist who emphasizes business development for small and medium-sized, closely held businesses. Many companies view employer-sponsored benefit and retirement plans as essential when it comes to recruiting and retaining top talent.

Each discipline complements the other when a larger organizational ecosystem exists within the CPA firm's wealth management division. As you fully implement client development within financial services, it enhances the traditional accounting business.

Winter arrives when you have made significant progress in developing most of your client base. In this season, you will need to decide if you should expand by allocating resources to further develop the business cycle. This could require adding more specialists to the financial services team to focus on even narrower categories within the financial services disciplines.

For example, you could add a Property and Casualty Agent along with a Life, Health, and Disability Insurance Agent. A Retirement Income Specialist, separate from the Employer-Sponsored Retirement Plan Specialist, could also prove instrumental. One could handle advisory and brokerage equity and fixed-income investment accounts while the other focuses on other retirement income asset management strategies, such as annuities.

You could further refine financial planning to incorporate two specialists representing that discipline. One could focus on advanced cases for higher net worth clients. The other could concentrate on greater-volume, shorter-duration engagements for the client base's broader spectrum.

The cycle could begin all over again with future CPA office mergers and acquisitions. The firm would bring in the next generation of Financial Professionals to reach the next generation of clients. These practitioners would accentuate rapport and relevance in perpetuating the business cycle.

Considerations for the Financial Professional

The CPA's job is to collaborate with you in discerning the seasons for the CPA firm and the financial services practice. As the Financial Professional, your job is to provide the leadership needed to successfully navigate those seasons. You bear the responsibility of laying out and executing a business development plan. Through dialogue and timely reporting, you must maintain communication on an ongoing basis.

In the spring season of the business cycle, the Financial Professional provides leadership by assembling a team to launch the mission. Like a musical group that begins with a few basic instruments and a modest technical crew, a tightly knit financial services group achieves maximum cohesion and efficiency. Each employee must rely on the others with the utmost confidence. Start with a small circle of individuals who have worked well together in the past, such as a Financial Professional, an Administrative Assistant, and an Administrative Clerical Assistant.

The practice can achieve a high success rate as the initial wave of business gets underway. Strategically begin the practice's spring season by conducting business with the CPAs for their own financial service needs. This showcases the processes and systems you have in place. It also affords the CPAs firsthand knowledge of the business. This adds credibility as they approach their own clients about financial services.

Spring gives way to summer, and the financial services practice is up and running at an increasing pace. You reach efficiencies as business becomes more robust. Summer often represents the most profitable season of the cycle. Revenue increases and surplus margins justify the initial start-up expenses. A familiarity in operations leads to a greater ease of doing business, and the multiplier effect kicks in.

Aspiring for higher levels of performance provides the driving force behind the summer season. As profitability increases, so will the opportunities to hire additional personnel. Understaffing could potentially disrupt business momentum, so take steps toward recruiting new Financial Professionals and administrative support personnel.

As autumn approaches, you begin to integrate these new team members. This can create a short-term reduction in profits as increased expenses occur. The practice can eventually generate higher revenues as these new Financial Professionals drill down deeper within their area of expertise for increased client development. Clearly explain to your clients the role of each Financial Professional. That way, they can experience a level of comfort and trust in working with the entire group.

A greater sense of teamwork exists as the specialized roles of the Financial Professionals complement one another. As you observe them collaborating with increased precision, communicate this progress with the CPAs and all support staff. Emerge as a leader to provide the structure and guidance needed to forge ahead with this expanded model.

When the scope and magnitude of business begins to diminish, winter has arrived. A cross-shadow of summer, winter presents new considerations involving the opportunity cost of time and money. Will you find it worthwhile to invest in the additional staffing and resources required to get to the next level? The leadership must agree to the best path going forward.

As in nature, atrophy occurs unless a new dynamic gets added. Not progressing may intrinsically result in going backward. For example, clients die and their beneficiaries receive their assets. This results in fewer assets under management. Clients spend money, resulting in a drawdown of account values. Advancement is necessary to ensure the long-term viability of the practice. For this to take place, consider adding Financial Professional Specialists, support staff, and the next generation of participants to make sure the mission progresses.

Based on the initial type of business the founders emphasized, each financial services practice will develop at its own pace. And each practice possesses a unique personality. Therefore, each of the four season's occurrence—and their duration—materializes differently for every practice. Strive to understand how the changing seasons impact your group and plan accordingly.

Commentary

The first year of financial services business within the CPA firm resembles a honeymoon season. Everything is new. A sense of enthusiasm prevails as CPAs refer clients for financial services, and Financial Professionals refer clients for accounting services. At this point in the cycle, the firm maintains a low expense structure. Therefore, profitability will appear higher than it will once growth requires expenditures toward more support staffing, office equipment, and supplies. This season represents spring.

The CPA's clients respond favorably regarding their most trusted advisor, the CPA, offering financial services in the same location where they have received reliable accounting advice. This also reinforces the financial services clients' perception that the firm is providing all services at the highest level of professionalism.

During the spring season, a simple mention of financial services in conversation with clients, a timely introduction of a strategic partner, and a little bit of enthusiasm are all it takes to make this work. Clients display an eagerness to discuss financial services needs they have already perceived for themselves, and they express an openness to the additional insight you can provide. Many will offer valuable input for improvements based on financial services they have received elsewhere. The practice conducts robust business creating the need for more support staff.

In the next few years, business continues to thrive from partner referrals, client referrals, and repeat business generated from periodic client review meetings. The team model can broaden out to include new financial services specialists to allow for greater expertise and more in-depth business development. This season is like summer.

Business consulting activity may increase for the accounting firm based on referrals from the financial services group. Business owners and higher-net-worth clients cultivated from financial services clients may require more advanced advice. This can result in valuation work for the CPAs.

Some businesses may want to outsource some traditional business management and administrative roles to the accounting firm on a contracted basis to reduce payroll expenses and employee liability. As this occurs, the accounting practice may also see the need to specialize and hire additional staff, such as a Payroll and Bookkeeping Specialist for closely held business clients.

As the business develops deeper and wider, expenses increase to support the growing demand. Percentages of profitability may decline, but the volume of profitability may increase.

The next cycle is like autumn. The firm sustains quality activity but with fewer new referrals from CPAs and Financial Professionals as they have already accessed most of their client base. You could describe autumn as the most efficient season, since periodic client review meetings generate the bulk of the new business.

The autumn season allows for going deeper into advanced business development, such as estate planning, business succession planning, and other matters that may require more time to develop for the client. During this phase of the cycle, it is vital to keep things fresh for clients and enhance current services.

Financial planning engagements and integrated client websites—that serve as a ready resource for client involvement and additional business development—may become more relevant during this time. Client Blueprints that map out meeting discussion topics and provide ongoing focus can also prove useful.

One more phase of the business cycle is the winter season. Long-standing clients and partners may retire or relocate. Prior generations of clients introduce successor generations in the transition of estate assets and business interests. In this season, develop new professional partner relationships to continue the legacy your firm has built with tireless effort and great care. Welcome younger CPAs and Financial Professionals into the firm for business sustainability and continuity of services. Their effort in reaching their peers is essential to the firm cultivating business relationships with subsequent generations of clients.

You may experience a sense of closure—as well as a fresh beginning—as you sustain activity in new ways. Technology advancements and style variations will shift the way you conduct business. And each generation will proceed differently. It is essential to embrace change with respect to the partnership's preferences and those of an ever-evolving client base.

Op-Ed

Seasons are circular. Where are we now, and where are we going?

In the honeymoon phase of the partnership, the firm experiences an abundance of new business generation. The CPA partners with the greatest "buy-in" move consistently through their client contacts to get the word out that the practice now offers financial services. They enthusiastically make introductions based on their confidence both in the financial services team and the venture itself.

Many CPAs feel a sense of pride in standing out from their peer firms by offering accounting and financial services under the same roof. Most of them quickly realize the benefit of added revenue that requires little effort on their part other than generating client referrals. The passive and recurring revenue from the financial services business comes as a welcome alternative to the demanding income production derived from time-intensive accounting and audit work.

At some point, these "champion" CPA partners will have covered the circuit for their client base. This allows other CPA partners to get in the game. Their warmup involves developing a higher belief level and increased skill at making client referrals. The observed success of their associates—along with a little positive peer pressure—goes a long way in ramping up business development for this group.

These CPA partners may have initially hesitated because they perceived the business venture could pose a risk to their client relationships. They may have displayed a subtle avoidance or even an open resistance. Developing a rapport with these CPAs can present a challenge for the Financial Professional. But as the Financial Professional applies a balance of persistence and patience, the effort invested can prove worthwhile. These CPA partners often step up to accelerate business and sustain it for an extended period of time.

The last group of CPAs represents those who may have completely rejected the initial inception of the strategic partnership. They may have cast a dissenting vote when the majority decided to introduce financial services as a CPA firm offering. Perhaps they voiced a concern about a perceived compromise of independence, or they simply may not have felt comfortable offering a new, unconventional business line in a traditional accounting tax practice.

It is also possible that these partners had loyalties and preferences for other Financial Professional candidates when the partners were conducting nominee interviews. Developing a financial services business with the selected Financial Professional could cause them to lose clients and centers of influence they had established in the industry. While they may wait the longest before joining in, they will have conclusively "counted the cost," and could eventually shine as the best at business development.

Just as a varying range of receptivity can emanate from the CPAs, the same applies to clients. Their responses can stretch from those who display an eagerness to discuss financial services to those who won't even consider the notion. As with the CPAs, the same progression of participation occurs based on perception. Those who quickly perceive the concept as a top-level practice offering both financial and accounting services, find a natural fit. Once again, persistence coupled with patience—regardless of the reason for hesitation—marks the best approach.

As time goes on and the client base grows, the financial services practice will develop an increasing percentage of new business from existing clients. This includes the further development of existing business, such as investment accounts with additional assets under management. Insurance reviews may expose the need for clients to increase their current coverage or improve their coverage values. Financial planning may identify opportunities for more financial planning. Client review meetings can prove instrumental in uncovering areas of need that the Financial Specialists would develop.

As a Financial Professional, if you establish a sustainable referral network, it can last well into the future. You can proliferate the business cycle beyond the life of the current client relationship to extend to their children, grandchildren, business partners and successors, friends, neighbors, and coworkers. Conceivably, there should never be a time when the firm lacks business development.

Be sure to adequately staff the financial services team during cycles of change to ensure a positive client experience. Coach your team members in the art of effective client communication. Train all staff to recognize new business opportunities based on client interaction and observed client activity. A change of address, beneficiary change, marital status change, or new employment uncovered in the process of updating client files can lead to subsequent business development. Often, the employees managing these records are the ones who discover new points for client discussion.

The Client Experience Specialist maintains a frontline position in identifying essential talking points for client meetings. Contact this team member daily so they can relay what they have observed during their client interactions.

Contact other staff members on a weekly basis to discuss client data that can lead to business development. As the business matures, this becomes even more essential since less business comes from new relationships, and more comes from existing relationships.

It is important to identify the season that the practice is currently experiencing. Effective communication from the leadership regarding the business cycles provides clarity and helps sustain business development and service.

The Details

When the CPA partners supply a stream of referrals, and new business activity maintains a vigorous pace, the spring season is in full bloom.

It's a healthy sign when the practice is conducting so much business that you must implement compensation tracking. If your firm's partners have obtained financial services licensing, you will need to establish "split rep" codes. Some financial companies charge a specified amount for each split rep code. The more partners, the more split rep codes. It's a good problem to have.

A little friendly competition for recognition and compensation can serve as a motivator for the partners. However, it can also produce contention. When the first-year, honeymoon halo effect starts to give way to the realities of managing a progressive and thriving business, personality differences and prior frictions can surface.

All organizations contain some element of drama. When you observe potentially divisive or counterproductive behavior, communicate this directly to the CPA managing partners. Chances are good they are well aware of what seems to be a newly detected phenomenon by the recently established Financial Professional. In other words, it's old news to them. Listen to the input provided by the CPA firm's senior management for how to manage these dynamics as it pertains to the financial services business. Beyond that, maintain an awareness that it exists and strive to keep processes moving along. Most of the time, the element of friction resolves itself in the end.

In the process of adding staff, you will discover that new hires don't always work out as anticipated. The initial role assignment may not provide the best fit, but another position could. Sometimes, it is the role itself, and not the employee, that is flawed. Well-meaning Financial Professionals who create a role assignment in the organization's early stages may later observe that it requires modification. (We're all making it up as we go along, to some degree.) But that's what makes this work exciting. As someone once said, the only thing you can dissect is something dead.

The financial services' environment is fluid and advancing, so expect a measure of trial and error.

You may hire an employee only to later discover that they don't provide the right fit for that position. If you don't have another assignment, you must tactfully communicate this to the employee. In some cases, the employee may sense the same thing and feels relieved when you bring it to light. Extend benevolence by providing a character reference for them and helping them find employment elsewhere.

The employee's termination could, however, leave them feeling rejected and frustrated. As the Financial Professional, you must prioritize what best serves *all* staff members and the company at large. Having to correct the departing employee's misguided efforts could adversely affect the remaining employees. The ongoing damage control campaign could cause problems for clients and CPA partners. The potential for damage and loss would represent too great a risk to retain that employee.

In addition to staffing choices, you will need to make decisions on other fronts as seasons change. How big is big enough? Do revenue goals justify the additional expenditure of time, money, and energy? Are new lines of business needed to round out the financial services offering?

These are just a few of the questions to ask and answer. But the questions do not present themselves in a vacuum. They surface within the flow of business execution. For most Financial Professionals, the answers lie in moving along with the current that presently propels the practice forward.

Details that surface in the second season of the practice often pertain to more advanced business development. This occurs when the CPAs refer their A+ clients. The CPAs usually won't take this step until they have verified the success of the financial services practice, and the quality of work and integrity of the Financial Professional. This season of the business cycle represents when the CPAs finally refer their top clients.

This provides a welcome challenge for the Financial Professional, who has worked hard just to make it this far. The referral itself represents high praise on the part of the referring CPA. As the Financial Professional, you may need to access additional resources to succeed in this endeavor. Collaborate with the advanced business development specialists at the financial company with which the firm has partnered and where the business most likely will be placed. Diligently resource these specialists as they can assist you in bringing about the intended new business.

When you acquire an exceptional case, don't appear too eager or anxious in the eyes of the referring CPA partner. The case may, indeed, present a learning opportunity. Make sure this doesn't appear blatantly obvious. If you don't possess the information or strategy required, simply acknowledge your intent to develop more mastery of the topic before working with the client. Advanced cases often require more of your time, so don't neglect providing quality service and attentiveness to your existing customary cases. You may need to consider hiring more support staff and additional Financial Professional Specialists during this phase of the growth cycle. This allows you and the newly added associate Financial Professionals to develop the more advanced cases.

With mutual participation, mutual compensation must follow. You can split smaller accounts with an associate Financial Professional. They would assume more responsibility in the day-to-day servicing, but they would still include you in the overall account management.

You can assign a Retirement Plan Specialist to handle the time-intensive, off-site work of developing and managing an employer-sponsored retirement plan. An Insurance Specialist can take leadership in different lines of insurance, including life, disability, long-term care, and health coverage. If the firm pursues property and casualty insurance coverage, you can add a Property and Casualty Insurance Specialist to cover that business line as well.

Investments and annuities have similar characteristics as growth and income assets, so the Investment Specialist may initially focus on both categories. Later, you can establish different Investment Specialists who separately focus on either managed advisory and brokerage investment portfolios, or annuities. You normally add the team members and support personnel for those disciplines over the course of several business cycles.

In the second or third season of the practice, you could incorporate financial planning. By that time, the client base has matured, and you are able to focus on that aspect of the business. The percentage of new business growth wanes, but business from the existing client base continues to grow.

Depending on the CPA firm's geographical areas and cultural inclinations, fee-based planning could become a top priority and the discipline on which you form your practice. In other settings, investment asset and insurance risk management may drive initial business development and allow you to add financial planning later on. Some firms lead with financial planning from the beginning because the client base or the leadership's preferences mandated it. When that's the case, all the other disciplines will subsequently develop from financial planning.

Adding financial planning in a subsequent season of the business cycle can create the opportunity for you to approach existing clients with additional services. Often, the first business relationship you establish with a client is an investment account or an insurance policy. With that established relationship, you can introduce financial planning as another essential part of financial services. Financial planning helps the client to better understand the context for other financial services and products, thus producing more opportunities for development.

It makes sense to begin with financial planning; however, the client may initially focus more on investing against current and future risk. Building success and trust can construct a platform for discussing financial planning services at the right time.

As a client becomes more interested in financial planning, you would include the Financial Planning Specialist for further discussion. As the referring Financial Professional, you should expect to remain involved in the early client meetings to maintain familiarity and continuity. The Financial Planning Specialist can build credibility with the client as the business case takes shape. As you introduce financial planning one client at a time, you can establish a reach across the client base that continues into subsequent seasons.

As your practice continues to expand, opportunities may surface outside the current CPA structure. This could take the form of peer CPA groups opting to outsource their practices' financial services to your group. This can lead to additional business merger and acquisition discussions between the two accounting firms. Expansion can also occur through alliances you form with professionals of other disciplines. You may network with business and estate attorneys who would be open to outsourcing their financial services business to you.

These potential business partners would need to pursue the proper licensing required for mutual business participation and compensation. Beyond the basic cost of licensing, they would find it cost-efficient to partner with your practice for financial services as it eliminates expenses they would normally incur, such as salaries, continuing education, and professional liability insurance.

Some states do not permit attorneys to become licensed to engage in financial services. Regulations in those states do not allow for "multi-disciplinary practices." It would be important to confirm the capacity in each state to allow active participation by attorneys in those locations to conduct financial services business.

The first two seasons of business development provide the platform for potentially expanding the business to new venues. So, it is important to maximize opportunities during those seasons to build strength and breadth before going into the next phase of the business cycle.

The next seasons of the practice cycle may be truly divergent and could involve buying other financial services businesses. Financial services groups' founding partners often develop their practices with current revenue in mind but with no firm exit strategy for retirement or business disposition. Your firm's senior leadership should consider approaching these peer firms to discuss buying out their existing practice. This could take the form of a simple lump sum buyout, or a staged buyout.

Another event that defines the progression of the practice is the retirement of key personnel, such as the founding Financial Professional. If this practitioner has been held in high regard, they should plan to remain in place for a few years. In a seamless transition, the successor Financial Professional could go in as a split-rep on existing accounts, or as a joint agent of record on existing insurance policies. This provides continuity for the client regarding account management and additional business development.

Half of the revenue for the residual advisory fees or commissions from the account would go to the retiring Financial Professional for current compensation, and the other half would go to the successor Financial Professional, who would use that revenue to make payments for a staged buyout of the retiring Financial Professional.

You would relieve the retiring Financial Professional of the work and overhead expenses required for maintaining their clients' investment accounts, annuity contracts, and insurance policies while still paying them commissions for an agreed-upon time. The retiring Financial Professional can then remain in place and enjoy a semiretired status while their successor develops a favorable relationship with the clients. This arrangement helps ensure conservation of the client base.

The fresh perspective offered by the successor Financial Professional would likely generate new business with existing clients. If the firm purchased the exiting Financial Professional's book of business, this would justify payments the firm made in agreement with the terms of the business buyout. This could prove profitable early in the acquisition phase.

This cycle of the practice could involve numerous transitions of participants. Based on the tenure of the founding Financial Professional, associate Financial Professionals and the support staff, the sequence of transition must be managed well. The firm can safeguard existing business, make new introductions, and develop additional business.

As next-generation Financial Professionals and Administrative Assistants are added, you can enter an enjoyable time of mentoring and apprenticeship. The retiring Financial Professionals and Administrative Assistants can pass along years of knowledge and experience to the new associates. This allows for business continuity and a preservation of beneficial relationships.

CHAPTER 12

Cultivating a Successful Business Continuation Plan and Exit Strategy

Considerations for the CPA

Over time, the financial services business matures and becomes self-sustaining. You begin to view it as more than just a revenue generator; it's an asset that adds value to your accounting practice.

To enhance that value, you can expand the practice through ongoing business development. The financial services practice could serve as a source of liquidity if the need arose for additional capital to bolster the accounting firm. You could also choose to sell and transfer a partial or entire ownership interest as a means of retirement income.

Alternatively, you could subsidize a buyout over time through the financial services business as part of an exit strategy. You could sell it outright to another CPA partner, a member of the financial services group, or an outside party. Communication within the strategic partnership would prove essential to reach an agreement regarding a transaction of this nature.

If you operate as a single practitioner, you may elect to hold onto your interest as a means of retirement cash flow. If a successor for the business is in place, this individual's eventual ownership participation could ensure their full commitment to the practice's continued business development.

If you operate within a multi-partner practice, you could similarly consider transferring interest among the CPA partners. A provision may exist in the partnership agreement allowing partners to sell interest shares at a designated age. This would allow for a clearly identified transition of ownership and first right of refusal—and makes for an orderly *business succession plan*.

Involve the Financial Professional in any discussion regarding selling the practice to an outside party. Consider them for first right of refusal before you approach an outside interest. You and the Financial Professional may discuss a total buyout that would further support business continuation.

Considerations for the Financial Professional

Your partnership interest in the financial services group represents both an asset and an income source. The same agreements for the CPA may also be in place for the Financial Professional.

If you offer to sell your shares of ownership, determine if a first right of refusal is in place for the CPA firm. If other Financial Professionals work within the group, the firm could establish a buyout (or buy-in) agreement.

Transfer for valuable consideration could represent an excellent tool for a successor/next-generation Financial Professional. This could involve a staged buyout derived from the revenue currently generated by the successor, who continues to assume more of a primary role. This individual would begin to take ownership of your duties as they develop client familiarity, contributing toward a seamless transition.

During the transition process, as the retiring Financial Professional you could oversee client relationships while assuming more of a consulting position. However, you could maintain a key role with select clients who might require a longer transition. This would ensure that these clients develop a favorable rapport with the new Financial Professional.

Differentiate your role from your successors to permit clients to establish a connection with their new Financial Professional. Similarly, the successor should respect your position as a changing of the guard unfolds.

You may choose to work part-time as a consultant for a specified period. Your years of hard-earned wisdom could provide your successor with the insight they need to avoid making costly mistakes as well as execute strategic decisions. Timely introductions and networking opportunities could enhance key business relationships in the industry and the community. This would ensure that the successor Financial Professional establishes a firm footing in building an enduring legacy for the practice.

The perspectives between generations may differ, but the essential components of sound business practices remain constant. The transition represents a time to draw from past experiences while sowing new seed—a time to teach and a time to learn. Overall, it's a time to ensure the successful continuation of the strategic partnership's mission.

Commentary

The CPA and the Financial Professional may consider a narrower focus for business continuation and succession. In this scenario, one generation follows another with the prospect of a business buyout based on the revenue the successor generates and sustains. The senior partners transfer a portion of their client servicing to the younger partners. The firm pays revenue to the retiring senior partners for meaningful involvement within a reduced workload capacity. These partners can make essential introductions and provide support as the younger partners take on more responsibilities. Senior partners may assume an extended role if all parties agree it would help maintain the practice's viability until the transition of leadership fully occurs.

However, sometimes the retiring partner doesn't know when to call it quits. They may find it hard to separate from a work routine they have established for many years. Since retirement for dedicated professionals can extend beyond the traditional social security age, the firm's leadership could help determine the retirement date. This avoids a potentially awkward situation, promotes clear understanding, and assures readiness for the transition by all participants. Team members can enjoy the experience with a clear demarcation of time and resources and a sense of closure.

Succession leadership and support staff can cast a vision as the life cycles of the firm perpetuate. Younger generations may consider establishing an advisory role for older generations to gain insight for best practices. They can minimize mistakes by learning from those who have successfully navigated through smooth streams as well as choppy waters.

The next generation's leadership can implement time-honored and proven principles into a contemporary structure as technological innovations and regulatory updates drive business trends. This generation of professionals will allow some traditions to fade away, while improving upon others. They will put their mark on the firm just as the prior generation did. All the while, the well-executed business succession plan quietly transports business into the future.

Op-Ed

Start with an end in mind. End with a start in mind.

A high probability of success can exist for CPAs and Financial Professionals who skillfully implement a financial services entity within a CPA firm. The business model mutually benefits CPAs and Financial Professionals with proven credibility and profitability. Who wouldn't want to participate in such an endeavor? As a practitioner, if client satisfaction and professional fulfillment describe your primary goals, this model offers great potential.

A unique characteristic of this business is that no minimal start-up costs are involved. No need exists for inventorying merchandise or for a revolving credit line to purchase products. You don't have to concern yourself with high shipping and storage costs or tight deadlines for customer delivery. Licensing, additional errors and omissions insurance, payroll for essential staffing, and minimal office equipment are the only initial expenditures. By sheer means of push and enterprise—with any measure of success—the firm can quickly recover the initial investment. The biggest outlay comes in the form of individual effort expended in speaking with clients to generate referrals that lead to business development.

Once progress begins, the firm will need to consider the direction of the financial services business. Initially, it could simply meet clients' needs and generate additional revenue for the firm. As it matures, it can build value for the firm's shareholders. The accounting firm's equity value may increase based on its stake in the financial services business.

A critical factor for the practice's valuation is the extent to which revenues could recur each year. Suppose the firm engages in broker/dealer business, such as variable annuities, variable life insurance, the sale of mutual funds, stocks, and bonds for commissions. In that case, the partners would heavily base the value of the business on the amount of initial and residual income generated.

Financial planning and fee-for-service fees vary. A few may involve fees that never increase or decrease from the amount designated in the first year. Many involve more fee generation for the first year than for subsequent years. Insurance commissions, by contrast, most often apply more compensation in the first year and a lesser, trailing commission in the following years.

The firm provides separate and distinct calculations for the practice's various disciplines. The advisory business may receive a valuation multiple of two or three times annual gross revenues. Commission-based broker/dealer and fixed insurance business may receive a valuation multiple of one or one-and-a-half times annual gross revenues. The financial planning business depends on the amount of recurring revenue involved and may receive a valuation multiple of up to one- or two-times revenue. The point is that value is created. Leadership should consider this when raising the next generation of participants.

Historically, the accounting industry considers it an admirable accomplishment for an accountant to "make partner." Commitment to industry standards, exemplary leadership qualities, and unquestionable integrity must be demonstrated by any candidate. The same can be said for Financial Professionals. The younger generation of practitioners should display these same essential attributes to ensure the firm's future viability.

A clear track should exist for professional advancement within the firm. Prospective partners should never feel the need to go elsewhere to climb the ladder of success. Opportunities should abound for those who exhibit the qualities the firm is willing to reward.

Senior leadership should keep an eye out for an aspiring new CPA partner who might seek to purchase an interest in the CPA firm. Attainment of partnership status may take the form of cash payment or from "sweat equity" through excellence and merited effort. Their purchase could also involve gaining a stake in the financial services group. Or that could present itself as a subsequent transaction. Either way, the opportunity provides an additional incentive for CPA successors to play an active role in the financial services group's ongoing business development. The CPA firm's partnership agreement could include a staged buy-in when the senior partners are bought out as the new partners buy in.

Often, a Financial Professional may have previously owned an interest in a financial services practice that was obtained when that book of business or client base was initially purchased by the firm. As part of the buyout, the Financial Professional could have become an Income Partner. This would involve a payout over time at retirement from the ongoing revenue of the practice instead of an initial cash purchase for value of the prior financial services business.

The firm would still formally recognize this as a type of partnership status. And it could ideally serve as part of a buyout. This would apply if a Financial Professional operated a financial services practice before the inception of the CPA firm partnership, and they brought their book of business with them into the firm. In this case, the CPA firm would oversee the payout of the retiring Financial Professional with no additional dilution of equity value for the existing partners.

The firm can extend financial incentives to the next generation of Financial Professionals by offering them Income Partner status with no current outlay of capital from the CPA partnership. Since compensation occurs at retirement, the firm's outflow would transpire once the candidate has fulfilled the participation requirements. Often, the firm will want to ensure the newer partner's optimal involvement and will require a specified number of years of service and revenue production. All of this involves an *internal* succession plan and business continuation.

If the CPA firm sells the business to an *outside* party, new considerations would come into play. Negotiations must assure that the new owners honor existing business continuation and buyout agreements. For example, CPAs would be grandfathered in for existing agreements and for new agreement terms going forward.

The new owners should also include proper recognition of interest in the financial services practice. As a CPA, exercise skill in negotiating while you are constructing the merger or purchase deal; this is the most opportune time to craft your desired terms. The acquiring firm is more apt to extend flexibility now rather than later when the inevitable challenges of integration unfold, and a greater demand is placed on their time, money, and energy. As always, seek business legal counsel in coming to terms with the acquiring firm.

As a Financial Professional, you should likewise seek representation at the negotiation table for previously established and future agreements. If the acquiring firm possesses its own financial services and financial company affiliations, you must allow for business interruptions and a potential loss of revenue while you form new agreements.

The firm should perform due diligence when establishing any new employment structure. Roles between the old firm's Financial Professionals and those of the new firm may overlap or even duplicate efforts. Territorialism can become an issue regarding "who does what" for leadership responsibilities and production. It is essential for Financial Professionals to remain in close communication with the CPA firm's senior leadership once it becomes apparent that a merger will occur. The Financial Professionals' industry knowledge could lend insight into critical details otherwise overlooked by the CPA firm.

For example, the new firm may not have a selling agreement with the same financial service companies as the existing firm. As a result, you may not be able to conduct some types of business as you have in the past. The new firm's financial institutional affiliations may prove less advantageous in some ways and more advantageous in other ways. As the CPAs work out the terms with the acquiring firm, you, as a Financial Professional can provide input that helps establish the most favorable outcome for all participants.

It could be the case that the acquiring CPA firm may choose *not* to offer financial services at all. This could provide the Financial Professional with the opportunity to buy the financial services practice outright from the existing partners. The firm could tie the terms of the buyout to a multiple of current anticipated cash flow value.

The CPAs should make a provision stating that account conservation and consistent, ongoing income are key factors in determining future payments. This ensures that you are paying a fair price. For the most part, you will make payments from the revenue received each year as you maintain the book of business.

The CPA partners who continue with the acquiring CPA firm may advocate to consider the purchase as an entity purchase to allow for optimal tax treatment of buyout payments. You would do well to obtain business legal counsel in forming a buyout agreement to determine the type of purchase that best serves your interests.

Since many financial services groups may possess few capital assets for consideration, the CPA partners would likely establish, by default, an entity purchase rather than an asset purchase. As the buyer, the acquiring firm would retain future liabilities in the case of an entity purchase, as prior business would continue into the future. Develop a clear understanding of both the risks and the rewards involved in purchasing the practice and servicing the current client base.

If you or your team purchases the financial services group, the CPA firm must establish new agreements for operations and business succession. The new entity name would likely no longer reflect a name that formerly referenced the CPA firm's name.

Locations could also change. If multiple CPA firm branch offices existed with business conducted in each office, operations may now take place from a single, centralized location. Acquiring additional office space as an "office of convenience" may become necessary for the financial services firm to maintain proximity to those locations and meet with area clients.

Staffing may change depending on the level of new business development and how the transition could temporarily diminish for personnel. For example, if the practice's current success has resulted from a substantial number of new referrals from the CPAs, you may experience a decline in the amount of business developed and maintained. Therefore, the practice may require less staffing.

On the other hand, if the practice has developed further into maturity where business development is less dependent on new client referrals from CPAs and more dependent on additional business from existing clients, staffing needs may continue as they were. In all cases, the entity value for the Financial Professional can grow.

A potential buyout by other existing partners or successor partners would be a key component for retirement considerations. Each existing partner must determine a retirement target date to prevent simultaneous retirement. If partners retire close to the same time, an interruption of cash flow could result as the firm makes payments to the departing partners while working to sustain business operations. Existing partners would have first right of refusal for a tender offer from a retiring partner.

An exception would be if an agreement existed to sell outright to an outside interest. In that case, simultaneous retirement could work well. Likely, you could work out an exit agreement over a specified time frame to allow management to transition to the successor partners. Retiring partners could agree to remain in support and advisory roles. You would recruit and train successor partners to allow for a measured level of involvement and experience.

The beginning is made with the end in mind. The beginning involved basic survival and potential supplementary income for the CPA partners. Later, the business can develop into a significant component of a sound retirement.

For the Financial Professional, a financial services business within a CPA firm creates a robust livelihood. After years of hard work, it can also produce significant retirement revenue. Both the CPAs and the Financial Professionals reap the benefits of a shared vision and entrepreneurial spirit for developing a successful financial services business.

The Details

The practice comes full circle as it progresses through each of the four seasons. In the springtime, details center around the scramble to put everything together. Review, revision, and adoption of the business plan provide the primary focal points. The CPAs' licensing and appointment or firm revenue flow processes follow the newly established practice's Operating Agreement and Partner Agreement. Business development training for the partners and staff leads to the financial services "machine" coming off the assembly line ready for production. This machine drives client referrals and new business development through the spring and summer seasons.

Additional staffing and team building accelerate through the second and third seasons, which are like summer and autumn. Acquiring additional financial services practices—and forming new strategic partnerships—may mark the autumn and winter seasons. With the maturing phase, or the winter season, creative destruction and reconstruction occurs. Current participants age out of the practice, making room for new producers and assistants.

The same meticulous attention to detail required for the entrance proves necessary for the exit. Agreements may exist for the retiring Financial Professional regarding business participation and splitting account fee revenue and commissions. To reflect the new split with the successor Financial Professional, the partners must update the split rep codes and co-broker agreements. They would also update financial planning agreements at the time of renewal or the onset of new financial plans or fee-for-service work.

If you are the retiring Financial Professional, you would mentor the new Financial Professional to promote success in all business disciplines.

You would conduct client review meetings with the successor Financial Professional in order to properly introduce them to clients. This communicates that the successor Financial Professional will assume more responsibility with proper deference by the retiring Financial Professional.

You would also train your successor in all aspects of client service. This establishes a hands-on familiarity with how things work and what the support staff expects the new Financial Professional to oversee. It is optimal for the existing support staff to remain in place during this transition.

You should observe best practices by providing ample notice before retiring or exiting the firm. This allows for timely planning and staffing. However, change can happen unexpectedly, and transitions and training may not transpire as you had intended. When that happens, communicate with partners, staff, and clients regarding possible interruptions and thank them in advance for their understanding and patience. Assure them that you are making every effort to ensure business continues with minimal interruption.

As the Financial Professional, you would provide more advanced notice of your departure than you would require of a support staff member who chooses to leave the company. If you have established a good rapport with each staff member, this would likely result in their communicating a resignation in a timely manner. When camaraderie exists among staff members, they embrace providing the extra training and support required of them in the wake of a staff member's exit.

It can be a monumental decision for a staff member to leave a position in a well-run firm, where they have enjoyed gainful employment and a sense of belonging. It is safe to assume that the departing team member gave considerable deliberation to this employment change.

Unfortunately, positive relationships don't always exist among staff members. And, as a Financial Professional, you may not catch every shift in an employee's mannerisms or a decrease in their productivity. In these instances, the departure of a team member may come as a surprise. Always strive to remain close to the pulse of your organization. This enables you to detect in advance the changes leading to an employee's resignation.

If the exit occurs on a favorable basis, allow adequate time for the new staff member's training and mentoring. Often, when a Financial Professional in a leadership role retires, their long-term support staff may simultaneously retire rather than exerting the start-up energy required to acclimate to new leadership.

Be sure to instill the same enthusiasm for production possibilities in the new Financial Professionals as you experienced as a first generation Financial Professional. Put in place the same perks and job satisfaction prospects. And, in addition to financial incentives, put forth a compelling rationale for employment and professional development. Make available to the new generation the same genuine camaraderie that the prior generation enjoyed.

Financial services is, indeed, *a service business*. Those who thrive in it are intrinsically service-oriented. For the producer, there must be match in ambition for increased commissions with a passionate mission to build strong client and staff relationships. The successor leadership must communicate this vision and develop the team involvement necessary to sustain the business model for long-term success.

The earlier generation should not make the mistake of frowning upon the culture of the newer generation. *They won't do it exactly like you did it.* Every generation has its own culture and serves a culture different from the prior one.

Some things never change, such as a high degree of professional knowledge and clear demonstration of client care. Many things, including how business is conducted and how people communicate, will change. A best practice is to respect the irrefutable differences between generations and agree that each can learn from the other.

When differences of opinion surface, suspend personal bias and exhibit open-mindedness. In the end, the generations may discover that they possess more similarities than differences. Finding common ground always represents an acceptable approach to building good rapport.

In times of crisis or disruption, input from cross-generational cycles may prove valuable. Sage advice from experienced, senior practitioners could be well-received by the incoming practitioners. And the younger generation's fresh perspective may be just what is needed to breathe new life into the practice. Often, what once was considered innovative is now deemed stale and routine. New energy and ideas are vital to continue the life cycle of the organization.

As the practice comes full circle and personnel and client transition occurs, the partnership leadership can be prepared. It's impossible to predict the future entirely, but strategic contingency planning should cover most foreseeable outcomes.

If there is a continuation of business, the established succession plan provides for the ongoing well-being of all participants. If the firm's central structure becomes altered, the continuing organization would absorb these operations according to the agreements in place. If a discontinuation of current culture occurs, work out the client base and business platform in the best interests of both the remaining and disengaging partners. Make it a goal to realize the fair value of the interests maintained. This would take place according to acceptable terms for those who would continue doing business, but in a different context.

The firm must continue to serve clients with the highest level of commitment and professionalism. All participants must be made whole for their efforts through the tendering of ownership interest shares for valuable consideration. The leadership should implement this so that it allows the remaining participants to sustain business and successfully execute the continuation plan.

In the final analysis, when it's done right, the end is only the beginning. Future generations will benefit as the organization continues to thrive.

Chapter Summaries

Chapter 1

Deciding to Offer Financial Services Through a CPA Firm

1. Only pursue CPA financial services if you really believe in the mission. You should possess a strong conviction that you are providing a skillfully executed, valuable service that will benefit your clients.

2. CPAs and Financial Professionals can partner together to provide complementary services and enjoy the benefits of achieving an optimal level of proficiency. Each can better leverage their time to promote top-level work within their respective disciplines.

3. CPAs can establish a lucrative business revenue stream by establishing financial services as part of their practice. It provides a passive way to boost profits without investing a significant amount of time.

Chapter 2

Developing a Proposed Business Plan for Financial Services

1. Present a written business plan that outlines the intended path forward for business development. When contending for a strategic business partnership, this could differentiate you from other candidates.

2. Devise a fluid business model that allows for business development changes as they occur. Don't base the business plan on unrealistic goals and objectives that produce inaccurate earnings projections.

3. Begin with a modest staffing model. Start small and grow from there.

Chapter 3

Finding the Right Fit for the CPA Firm and the Financial Professional

1. A shared culture represents the single most important key to a successful partnership. The CPA and the Financial Professional should possess similar values and leadership styles.

2. Birds of a feather flock together. You should enjoy working with the people with whom you co-labor. Choose a business partner with whom you can create a positive and profitable experience.

Chapter 4

Developing the Best Structure for Business

1. A formal partnership cements the business relationship between the CPA and the Financial Professional. The business entity structure provides a sturdy platform upon which to conduct business.

2. The firm leadership would need to choose how to pay each participant. Consider licensing for each partner if your entity consists of only a few partners. For larger entities with more partners, recognize profit at the entity level based on the percentages of ownership and the type of business conducted.

Chapter 5

Creating and Managing a Business Development System

1. The most essential component for success takes place when, as a CPA or a Financial Professional, you simply tell your clients that the CPA firm now offers financial services. You must convey a high belief level to effectively promote the business.

2. Accounting clients need to observe that the Financial Professional works in partnership with their most trusted advisor, the CPA. Clear collaboration must exist within the partnership.

3. Fully utilize the client management system.

Chapter 6

Establishing and Maintaining a Client Management System

1. Implement a user-friendly client management system that provides state-of-the-art data storage and client contact management.

2. Integrate all financial services team members into a centralized client support and communication system to sustain excellence in client services and new business generation.

Chapter 7

Pursuing Specialized Disciplines of Financial Services

1. In the beginning, start small with a few core competencies in developing the financial services business. Over time, add specialists to allow for greater expertise in business development.

2. As business and revenue build, continue to add support personnel and specialists to promote higher levels of excellence and proficiency in the various financial services' disciplines.

Chapter 8

Financial Planning: To Fee or Not to Fee

1. Fee-for-service work provides a business niche that can set your firm apart from the competition. This discipline allows for an objective approach to a more advanced range of services that may appeal to higher-profile clients.

2. Financial planning complements the CPA firm's business model. It can lead to additional business in the other disciplines of financial services, such as investment asset management, insurance risk management, and employer benefit–plan management.

Chapter 9

Three Most Important Keys: Communication, Communication, Communication

1. Financial Professionals and CPAs must consistently communicate through a variety of media. This establishes rapport and helps to detect problems when they first surface.

2. Financial professionals must regularly communicate with their financial services team members to ensure an efficient flow of operations. CPAs and Financial Professionals must sustain formal and informal communication with clients to uncover new business opportunities and retain existing client accounts.

Chapter 10

Managing Seasons of Change

1. Prepare for the unexpected. Think through changes that could happen over time and establish effective contingency plans.

2. Discuss difficult topics pertaining to business continuity. This enhances participation and agreement among the partners and builds trust. Anticipate potential business disruption. That way, you can equip your team for readiness when these challenges take place.

Chapter 11

Understanding the Cycles of the CPA Firm Financial Services Business

1. Natural seasons of progression define a successful financial services group. Make a plan that identifies the cycles of the business so that, when seasons change, you have the right resources available to maintain a strong business model.

2. Embrace each season's arrival. When team members recognize and properly navigate the changing seasons, it contributes to a healthy progression of the practice.

Chapter 12

Cultivating a Successful Business Continuation Plan and Exit Strategy

1. It is important to plan for the business model's culmination. The business entity may continue, but the participants may transition. Identify the best possible outcome as these changes occur.

2. Identify potential successors for business continuation. Share with them your observations and expectations for developing a business succession plan. Cultivate a "buy-in" with these candidates to promote a smooth transition when the time arrives.

About the Author

In 1998, Billy Hemby took the idea of establishing a financial services group inside a CPA firm to Pittard Perry & Crone, Inc, a CPA firm in North Carolina. As founding managing partner, he collaborated with the tax partners to establish PPC Financial Group, LLC in December 2000. The entity quickly ramped up client service and revenue production upon the licensing of the partners for broker/dealer, registered investment advisor, and insurance business.

The firm merged with Regional CPA firm Carr Riggs & Ingram, LLC in 2013. At that time, the wealth management group merged with Level Four Group, LLC, the wealth management division of Carr Riggs & Ingram, LLC. Billy currently serves as managing director of Level Four Financial in North Carolina. The group has established an ensemble model of Financial Professionals who specialize in several core disciplines of financial services. Level Four's corporate objective is changing the future of financial advice through a holistic financial planning process. Billy enjoys helping CPAs and Financial Professionals in the shared pursuit of developing excellence in CPA Financial Services.

Outside of the office, Billy is active in community service. He is a Paul Harris Fellow in Rotary International. He has served as a district Club Leader of the Carolina Club in the General Alumni Association of the University of North Carolina at Chapel Hill. He is on the Advisory

Board of Barton College. He is a recognized member of the Order of First Families of North Carolina. He participates on the lay ministry team at St. Timothy's Episcopal Church in Wilson, North Carolina.

Billy enjoys competitive tennis since his first Junior Tournament in the United States Tennis Association (USTA) in 1976. He and his wife, Jan, make their home in Eastern North Carolina where his family's roots extend back over 300 years.

To find out more about financial services for a CPA firm or for consulting for your professional practice, call 866-834-1040 or email us at cpafs@levelfourgroup.com.

www.levelfourgroup.com/cpafs

Index

unexpected events and, 127

D

death, 26, 111, 118

decision-making communications, 99–100

deferred compensation payouts, 51–52

digital record storage, 68. *See also* client management system

E

earnings before interest and taxes (EBIT), 38–39, 130

economic cycles, weathering, 117, 119, 122, 128

email

  client communication via, 63, 68, 105, 111

  general discussion, 55–56, 107, 110

employee difficulties, 133–134, 167–168

employer benefit plan services, 62, 72, 76, 88, 175

Employer Benefit Plan Specialists, 74

Employer-Sponsored Retirement Plan Specialists, 138–139

ensemble model, 96

enthusiasm

  benefits of, 142, 144, 168

  general discussion, 12–13, 20–21, 73, 104

  proven systems versus, 23, 103

errors and omissions insurance, 47, 159

estate attorneys, 90, 131, 152

estate planning, 62, 84, 90

Event Planners, 75–76

exit strategy

  attention to detail needed, 166–170

  buyout agreements

    Income Partner status, 161–164

    internal plans, 160–162

    overview, 153–159

  considerations, 155–158

  general discussion, 177

  good relations during, 166–170

  internal continuity plans

    Income Partner status, 161–162

    professional advancement track, 26, 31, 79, 160–161

    valuation multiple considerations, 159–161

  part-time consulting, 157–158

  retirement, 130–133, 158–159

  selling to outside parties, 162–166

F

feedback

  from clients, 64, 105–106

  exchanging, 29, 32, 51, 132

fee-for-service financial planning. *See also* Financial Planning Specialists

  in business cycle, 151–152

  business structure, 47–49